Inventory Subsystem

- **Designing the Subsystem**
- **Recording and Processing**
- **Internal Control over Accounts Payable**
- **Inventory Recording and Measurement**
- **Inventory Subsidiary Ledger**
- **Managing Inventory**

This module is concerned with accounting for, and management of, inventory. We will examine the measurement of inventory and the recording of inventory transactions under the perpetual inventory system, together with internal controls and different systems for managing inventory levels.

For many trading and manufacturing businesses, inventory is a very significant asset. It can require a large investment of working capital and in modern times where cash is used less commonly, it is probably the most difficult asset to keep securely. It can also be difficult to manage inventory levels – a business needs to have sufficient inventory on hand to meet customer requirements, while not overstocking and wasting resources unnecessarily.

In the *Accounts Receivable* module of this course, the subsidiary ledger for accounts receivable was introduced. Subsidiary ledgers can also be used to record accounts payable and inventory. A separate **accounts payable ledger** allows us to keep accurate records of exactly how much is owed to each individual creditor, while at the same time maintaining a total creditors' balance in the **accounts payable control account** in the general ledger. A separate **inventory ledger** allows us to keep accurate records of the quantity and total cost of individual inventory items. At the same time a total inventory balance is maintained in the **inventory control account** in the general ledger.

This module discusses the desired outputs from the accounts payable subsystem and the internal controls that are necessary to keep inventory secure.

Previous courses have used the **periodic inventory system**. This method records purchases of inventory in an expense account (the *purchases* account) during the reporting period. At the end of the period purchases are adjusted for opening and closing inventory to calculate the cost of goods sold.

In this module we will adopt the **perpetual inventory system**, recording inventory as an *asset* until it is sold. When a sale takes place, the cost of those goods is transferred from inventory directly to a **cost of goods sold** *expense* account. The perpetual system has a number of advantages nowadays as it provides up-to-date records and is particularly well suited to computerisation.

We will also consider **measurement** of inventory. This is extremely important because the carrying amount of inventory affects both cost of goods sold (hence profit) and the total of current assets in the statement of financial position.

Designing the Subsystem

Financial information is produced by an **accounting system**. A system may be represented as:

ISBN: 9780170229845

The **input** is the daily transaction record of the business. Transactions relating to accounts payable are recorded on source documents such as purchase orders issued, invoices and credit notes received, cheque butts and bank statements.

The **process** is the classifying and recording of information in the journals and in the general and subsidiary ledgers. The information is then summarised in the trial balance.

The **output** is the financial statements – the income statement and statement of financial position.

Remember that an accounting system comprises a number of **subsystems,** each of which produces financial information about a specific area of the business. Accounting for inventory forms *part* of the overall accounting system. When we are designing an accounting subsystem, we must identify first the information that management will require for decision-making. We then start from the end – identify the *output* that will provide the required management information. Some questions that must be answered are:

- What reports do we want the subsystem to produce?
- What information is contained in those reports?
- Where will this information come from?

The list of objectives which follows will assist us in designing the subsystem. By determining the output required, we will once again be able to determine the input necessary and design a process which will convert that input into the output we need for making business decisions.

> To operate an accounting system that will:
> - allow the prompt and accurate processing of purchase requisitions
> - record credit transactions accurately through appropriate source documents and journal entries
> - process these transactions in ledger accounts and provide an up-to-date list of accounts payable
> - provide accurate records of GST to be claimed from the Inland Revenue Department
> - ensure that all credit purchases are properly authorised
> - maintain an adequate internal control system to prevent errors and fraud
> - maximise the firm's credit rating through an efficient system of processing accounts for payment
> - maximise the use of credit to reduce the cost of working capital
> - provide relevant and timely information to management for decision-making.

If the subsystem meets all of these objectives, the business will achieve the maximum benefits available from buying goods on credit, through minimising the use of business working capital to finance inventory while maintaining a good reputation with both customers and suppliers.

If we examine the subsystem objectives, the following required outputs of the subsystem can be determined:

- Total creditors (accounts payable control account)
- Details of each supplier's account (accounts payable ledger)
- Vouchers authorising payment (from accounts payable ledger)
- Details of GST to be refunded from the Inland Revenue Department (from the GST ledger account).

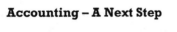

Accounting – A Next Step

ISBN: 9780170229845

Activities

1 How does the purchase of goods on credit minimise the working capital requirements of a business?

_____

_____

_____

_____

_____

2 **a** Explain why it is important that purchase orders should be processed **accurately**.

_____

_____

_____

_____

b Explain why it is important that purchase orders should be processed **promptly**.

_____

_____

_____

_____

_____

_____

3 Explain why credit purchases must be properly authorised.

_____

_____

_____

_____

_____

4 Explain why it is important that invoices from suppliers be processed and approved for payment promptly.

_____

_____

_____

_____

5 State whether the GST paid on purchases is an asset or a liability and explain your reasoning.

Asset / Liability

_____

_____

_____

Recording and Processing

Credit Purchases

The source document for a credit purchase is the original of a **Tax Invoice** which has been sent by the supplier. Tax invoices are discussed in detail in the *Accounts Receivable* module of this course. In the case of purchases, we are receiving these invoices rather than sending them. The source document for a purchase return or allowance is the original copy of a credit note sent by the supplier.

As we mentioned in the *Accounts Receivable* module, a credit purchase is initiated by a **purchase order**. This document is completed by the firm that is making the purchase and it is sent to the supplier. A typical purchase order is shown below.

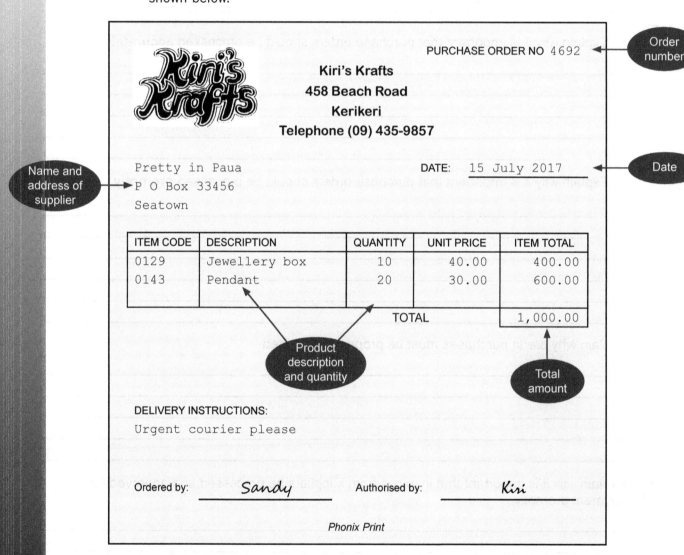

PURCHASE ORDER NO 4692 — Order number

Kiri's Krafts
458 Beach Road
Kerikeri
Telephone (09) 435-9857

Name and address of supplier →

Pretty in Paua
P O Box 33456
Seatown

DATE: 15 July 2017 — Date

ITEM CODE	DESCRIPTION	QUANTITY	UNIT PRICE	ITEM TOTAL
0129	Jewellery box	10	40.00	400.00
0143	Pendant	20	30.00	600.00
			TOTAL	1,000.00

Product description and quantity

Total amount

DELIVERY INSTRUCTIONS:
Urgent courier please

Ordered by: *Sandy*   Authorised by: *Kiri*

Phonix Print

Important!

- The order has a number. This ensures that all orders can be accounted for and no unauthorised ordering takes place. It also enables any queries to be dealt with easily. Large firms will often place a lot of orders with the same supplier. When the supplier sends the invoice, the order number is quoted on it so that the order and invoice can be matched before payment is approved.

 PHOTOCOPYING PROHIBITED

ISBN: 9780170229845

Important!

- The price of the goods is shown on the order. This is because the goods have probably been ordered from a catalogue. It also acts as a signal to the supplier that *Kiri's Krafts* is not expecting to pay more than $1,000 for this order. If the price charged is higher than this, *Kiri's Krafts* may withdraw the order. Finally, showing the price on the order enables the clerk who checks the invoice to have some idea of the price which the supplier should be charging for these particular goods. He or she will query the invoice if the two prices do not agree.

- No GST calculation is shown on the purchase order. Whether or not GST is included in the quoted price depends upon the conventions applying in that particular industry. Very often prices shown are GST exclusive.

- In a manual system, at least three copies are made of this order. The original copy is sent to the supplier and a copy is sent to the accounts department to await the arrival of the invoice. The third copy is retained in numerical order in the order book for future reference. Larger firms may require additional copies for various purposes.

- In large firms, the purchasing department will require a purchase requisition from the department placing the order. This must be authorised by the supervisor of the department concerned. In this way all orders are placed through a single purchasing department and it is possible to control the ordering of goods more effectively.

Control over Purchase Orders

It is very important that the issue of purchase orders is well controlled. Orders are numbered so that every one can be traced. In a manual accounting system, if an order is spoilt, all copies should be kept in the order book and it should be clearly marked 'VOID' or 'CANCELLED'. It is also very important that all new order books are securely locked away until required.

If these procedures are not followed, an opportunity for fraud arises. A member of staff may issue an untraceable order (either not numbered, or from a 'spare' book) and intercept the goods from the supplier as they arrive. To protect both the business and its staff, one important internal control is to separate the duties of issuing purchase orders and approving invoices for payment. This control can help prevent activities such as that described above, unless of course two members of staff are colluding with each other.

In a computerised environment, there is less likelihood that this situation would arise. Purchase orders are numbered automatically by the software. However, where a firm uses preprinted order forms, supplies of blank forms must be kept securely so that they cannot be stolen and used fraudulently.

The Perpetual Inventory System

In previous courses, inventory was recorded using the **periodic inventory system**. Under this system, the cost of goods sold was calculated at the end of the reporting period by taking opening inventory, adding purchases and other relevant expenses, and then deducting closing inventory. The carrying amount of the inventory at year-end was calculated using a physical count of inventory on hand.

In this course we are using a different system of recording inventory – the **perpetual inventory system**. Under this system, a continuous record of inventory on hand is maintained. When inventory is purchased, it is recorded as an **asset**. When inventory is sold, its cost is transferred to the **cost of goods sold** expense. We recorded these entries in the *Accounts Receivable* module of this course.

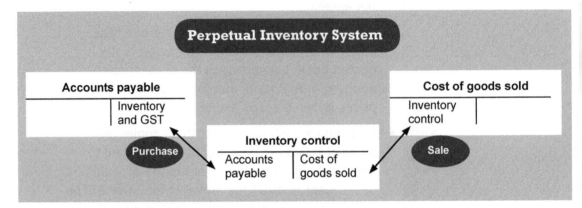

At any time, a theoretical record of the quantity and cost of the goods on hand is available. Since records are kept of all goods bought and sold, it is possible to calculate the gross profit without carrying out a stocktake, because the cost of goods sold is known at all times.

The book-keeping entries for the perpetual system are different from the periodic system. There are three major differences:

- There is no *purchases* account in the ledger. When goods are purchased they are still recorded in a purchases journal, but are *debited* to the **inventory** control account in the general ledger. Purchases returns and allowances are *credited* to the **inventory** control account.
- All sales must be recorded twice – at selling price and at cost price. When we recorded sales in the *Accounts Receivable* module, we also recorded the **cost of goods sold** and *credited* it to the inventory control account in the ledger.
- If a perpetual system is used, it is necessary to have a cost of goods sold column in the cash receipts journal to record the cost of cash sales.

The Purchases Journal

Credit purchases (and only **credit** purchases) are first recorded in the **purchases journal**. This is a *special journal* used to record one type of transaction, in the same way as a cash receipts journal is used only to record cash received. The purchases journal is designed to capture the relevant input into the accounting system from the invoices received by the firm.

Information needed to record all aspects of each purchase transaction is:
- the date of the transaction
- the name of the supplier
- the total amount of the invoice
- the GST component of the invoice.

ISBN: 9780170229845

Consider the following example:

Kiri's Krafts had the following credit purchases in October 2019:

Date	Supplier Name	Invoice No	Amount (inc GST) $
Oct 2	Colinette's Crafts	566	1,150
4	Flaxworks	215	1,035
14	Jill's Jewellery	356	805
20	Colinette's Crafts	572	598
21	Flaxworks	220	1,196
30	Jill's Jewellery	371	184

These are recorded in the purchases journal as follows:

		Kiri's Krafts					
		Purchases Journal					**Page 2**
Date		Particulars	Invoice No	Ref	Total	Inventory	GST payable
					$	$	$
Oct	2	Colinette's Crafts	566		1,150	1,000	150
	4	Flaxworks	215		1,035	900	135
	14	Jill's Jewellery	356		805	700	105
	20	Colinette's Crafts	572		598	520	78
	21	Flaxworks	220		1,196	1,040	156
	30	Jill's Jewellery	371		184	160	24
					$4,968	$4,320	$648
					320	**130**	**310**

Important!

- The purchases journal records the credit purchase of **goods**. Credit purchases of other items, eg property, plant and equipment, are recorded in the **general** journal.

- The source documents for preparing the purchases journal in a manual system are the original copies of the invoices from the suppliers.

- The invoice numbers in the purchases journal are not in consecutive order. This is because suppliers are using different invoice books which have different numerical sequences.

- The purchases journal records only **credit** purchases. Cash purchases are recorded in the **cash payments** journal.

- The posting reference for each column is shown below the total.

- No entries are made in the reference column at this stage. This column is used for posting to individual creditors' accounts in the same way as for accounts receivable.

Posting to the ledger

When using the perpetual inventory system, the purchases journal is posted to the inventory (asset) control account. We can represent this on the accounting equation as follows:

	A	+ Ex	=	L		+ Eq	+ I
	Inventory control			Accounts payable	GST payable		
Invoices received $4,968	+ 4,320		=	+ 4,968	− 648		
	Debit			Credit	Debit		

Ledger postings require the following entries:

Debit entries	$	Credit entries	$
Inventory control	4,320	Accounts payable	4,968
GST payable	648		
	$4,968		$4,968

GST of $648 has been invoiced. This will be claimed from IRD later.

We will post these entries to the ledger in the next section.

Purchases Returns and Allowances

Sometimes goods may be returned to suppliers because they are damaged or faulty in some way, or they may not be what was ordered. On these occasions, the firm will receive a **credit note** for the goods returned. Credit notes are recorded in the **purchases returns and allowances** journal.

Sometimes a credit note may be received for reasons other than the return of goods, such as overcharging by the supplier or as compensation for damaged goods. Since these events also affect the cost of inventory, they are entered in the purchases returns and allowances journal along with the return of goods.

Consider the following example:

Kiri's Krafts received the following credit notes in October 2019:

Date	Customer Name	Credit Note No	Amount (inc GST) $
Oct 4	Colinette's Crafts	254	184
16	Jill's Jewellery	442	92
24	Flaxworks	899	276

The purchases returns and allowances journal is as follows:

Kiri's Krafts						
Purchases Returns and Allowances Journal						Page 1
Date	Particulars	Credit Note No	Ref	Total $	Inventory $	GST payable $
Oct 4	Colinette's Crafts	254		184	160	24
16	Jill's Jewellery	442		92	80	12
24	Flaxworks	899		276	240	36
				$552	$480	$72
				320	130	310

Accounting – A Next Step

ISBN: 9780170229845

Posting to the ledger

When using the perpetual inventory system, the purchases returns and allowances journal is posted to the inventory (asset) account. We can represent this on the accounting equation as follows:

	A	+ Ex	=	L		+ Eq	+	I
	Inventory control			Accounts payable	GST payable			
Credit notes received $552	− 480		=	− 552	+ 72			
	Credit			Debit	Credit			

Ledger postings require the following entries:

Debit entries	$	Credit entries	$
Accounts payable	552	Inventory control	480
		GST payable	72
	$552		$552

GST!

GST of $72 has been credited back. This must be paid to IRD later because it was claimed from them when the goods were originally purchased.

We must credit the GST account in this instance, because the GST was recorded as an asset (or reduction in liability) when the goods were first purchased. Since the purchase did not actually eventuate, the GST cannot be claimed back and this must be reversed.

Sales and Sales Returns and Allowances

Recording sales and sales returns and allowances was covered in detail in the *Accounts Receivable* module of this course. During the month of October, *Kiri's Krafts* made total sales of $6,808 (including GST of $888) and the cost of goods sold was $3,826. A summary of the ledger postings (from SJ5) to record sales is:

Debit entries	$	Credit entries	$
Accounts receivable	6,808	Sales	5,920
Cost of goods sold	3,826	GST payable	888
		Inventory control	3,826
	$10,634		$10,634

Remember!

The entry to record cost of goods is exclusive of GST because the GST was recorded when the goods were first purchased.

Sales returns for October totalled $184 (including GST of $24). The cost of inventory returned was $100. All of the inventory was in good condition and returned to stock. The ledger postings to record sales returns (from SRJ1) are:

Debit entries	$	Credit entries	$
Sales returns and		Accounts receivable	184
allowances	160	Cost of goods sold	100
GST payable	24		
Inventory control	100		
	$284		$284

If the inventory that was returned had been damaged and was unsaleable, it would not have been returned to stock. Instead of being debited to the inventory (asset) account, it would be debited to an expense account: *inventory written off*. The ledger accounts for the above transactions are shown on the following pages.

Kiri's Krafts – General Ledger

Accounts receivable control — 120

Date	Particulars	Ref	$	Date	Particulars	Ref	$
Oct 1	Balance	b/d	8,119	Oct 31	Sales returns and allowances and GST	SRJ1	184
31	Sales and GST	SJ5	6,808				

Inventory control — 130

Date	Particulars	Ref	$	Date	Particulars	Ref	$
Oct 1	Balance	b/d	1,945	Oct 31	Accounts payable	PRJ1	480
31	Accounts payable	PJ2	4,320		Cost of goods sold	SJ5	3,826
	Cost of goods sold	SRJ1	100				

GST payable — 310

Date	Particulars	Ref	$	Date	Particulars	Ref	$
Oct 31	Accounts payable	PJ2	648	Oct 1	Balance	b/d	900
	Accounts receivable	SRJ1	24	31	Accounts payable	PRJ1	72
					Accounts receivable	SJ5	888

Accounts payable control — 320

Date	Particulars	Ref	$	Date	Particulars	Ref	$
Oct 31	Inventory and GST	PRJ1	552	Oct 1	Balance	b/d	3,600
				31	Inventory and GST	PJ2	4,968

Sales — 610

Date	Particulars	Ref	$	Date	Particulars	Ref	$
				Oct 1	Balance	b/d	41,880
				31	Accounts receivable	SJ5	5,920

Sales returns and allowances — 611

Date	Particulars	Ref	$	Date	Particulars	Ref	$
Oct 1	Balance	b/d	300				
31	Accounts receivable	SRJ1	160				

Cost of goods sold — 710

Date	Particulars	Ref	$	Date	Particulars	Ref	$
Oct 1	Balance	b/d	30,356	Oct 31	Inventory	SRJ1	100
31	Inventory	SJ5	3,826				

Remember!

When the perpetual basis of recording inventory is used, purchases returns and allowances are posted directly to the **inventory** control account in the ledger. There is no separate **purchases returns and allowances** account. If managers require information regarding purchases returns and allowances, a different set of entries would be required.

 PHOTOCOPYING PROHIBITED

ISBN: 9780170229845

Kiri's Krafts – General Ledger

Accounts receivable control — 120

Date	Particulars	Ref	Dr $	Cr $	Balance $
Oct 1	Balance	b/d			8,119 Dr
31	Sales and GST	SJ5	6,808		14,927 Dr
	Sales returns and				
	allowances and GST	SRJ1		184	14,743 Dr

Inventory control — 130

Date	Particulars	Ref	Dr $	Cr $	Balance $
Oct 1	Balance	b/d			1,945 Dr
31	Accounts payable	PJ2	4,320		6,265 Dr
	Cost of goods sold	SJ5		3,826	2,439 Dr
	Cost of goods sold	SRJ1	100		2,539 Dr
	Accounts payable	PRJ1		480	2,059 Dr

GST payable — 310

Date	Particulars	Ref	Dr $	Cr $	Balance $
Oct 1	Balance	b/d			900 Cr
31	Accounts payable	PJ2	648		252 Cr
	Accounts payable	PRJ1		72	324 Cr
	Accounts receivable	SJ5		888	1,212 Cr
	Accounts receivable	SRJ1	24		1,188 Cr

Accounts payable control — 320

Date	Particulars	Ref	Dr $	Cr $	Balance $
Oct 1	Balance	b/d			3,600 Cr
31	Inventory and GST	PJ2		4,968	8,568 Cr
	Inventory and GST	PRJ1	552		8,006 Cr

Sales — 610

Date	Particulars	Ref	Dr $	Cr $	Balance $
Oct 1	Balance	b/d			41,880 Cr
31	Accounts receivable	SJ5		5,920	47,800 Cr

Sales returns and allowances — 611

Date	Particulars	Ref	Dr $	Cr $	Balance $
Oct 1	Balance		300		300 Dr
31	Accounts receivable	SRJ1	160		460 Dr

Cost of goods sold — 710

Date	Particulars	Ref	Dr $	Cr $	Balance $
Oct 1	Balance	b/d			30,356 Dr
31	Inventory	SJ5	3,826		34,182 Dr
	Inventory	SRJ1		100	34,082 Dr

Note

The accounts receivable, accounts payable and GST accounts shown here are not complete. They would contain other entries for items such as cash receipts and payments, bad debts, discounts, interest and freight charges.

 PHOTOCOPYING PROHIBITED

ISBN: 9780170229845

Inventory Subsystem

13

Activities

 1 Listed below are the credit transactions of *Mystical Moments* for the month of July 2017. The firm is registered for GST on the invoice basis. All goods returned by customers were fit for resale.

Jul 1	Bought goods from *Leatherware*, $138, invoice no 201
4	*Super Souvenirs* bought goods, $345, invoice no 715 (cost of goods sold $180)
6	Returned goods to *Leatherware*, $23, credit note no 130
8	Bought goods from *Beautiful Candles*, $230, invoice no 611
10	Sold goods to *Karmic Krystles*, $736, invoice no 716 (cost of goods sold $400)
12	*Super Souvenirs* returned goods, $46, credit note no 904 (cost of goods returned $24)
14	Bought goods from *Leatherware*, $299, invoice no 245
15	Bought goods from *Magic Models*, $391, invoice no 897
16	Sold goods to *Karmic Krystles*, $621, invoice no 717 (cost of goods sold $320)
19	Returned goods to *Magic Models*, $69, credit note no 007
20	Bought shop fittings on credit from *Retail Supplies*, $2,530, invoice no 1954
21	*Karmic Krystles* returned goods, $115, credit note no 905 (cost of goods returned $60)
24	*Betta Books* bought goods, $322, invoice no 718 (cost of goods sold $210)
25	Sold goods to *Karmic Krystles*, $414, invoice no 719 (cost of goods sold $340)
26	Bought goods from *Leatherware*, $460, invoice no 291
28	Bought goods from *Magic Models*, $506, cheque no 179
29	*Betta Books* returned goods, $115, credit note no 906 (cost of goods returned $75)
30	Bought goods from *Beautiful Candles*, $184, invoice no 626
31	Sold goods to *Super Souvenirs*, $230, invoice no 720 (cost of goods sold $165)
	Returned goods to *Beautiful Candles*, $46, credit note no 451.

Opening ledger balances for the year beginning 1 July 2017 were:

Accounts receivable	$1,200 Dr	Accounts payable	$900 Cr
Inventory	850 Dr	GST payable	150 Cr

DO THIS!

a Identify any purchase transactions from the above list that would not appear in the purchases journal.
b State where each of the transactions you identified above would be recorded and explain in each case why they are not in the purchases journal.
c Prepare the purchases, purchases returns and allowances, sales and sales returns and allowances journals for *Mystical Moments*.
d Post the journals to the ledger accounts provided. (The chart of accounts references are given on the ledger accounts.) Balance the *inventory* and cost of *goods sold* accounts only.

a Identify any purchase transactions from the above list that would not appear in the purchase journal.

_____

_____

b State where each of the transactions you identified above would be recorded and explain in each case why they are not in the purchases journal.

_____

_____

_____

_____

c

Mystical Moments
Purchases Journal

		Inv no	Ref	Total $	Inventory $	GST payable $

Purchases Returns and Allowances Journal

		C/N no	Ref	Total $	Inventory $	GST payable $

Sales Journal

		Inv no	Ref	Total $	Sales $	GST payable $	Cost of goods sold $

ISBN: 9780170229845

Inventory Subsystem

c

Mystical Moments
Sales Returns and Allowances Journal

		Inv no	Ref	Total $	Sales returns & allow $	GST payable $	Cost of goods sold $

d

Mystical Moments
General Ledger

Inventory control   130

GST payable   310

Accounts payable control   320

Cost of goods sold   710

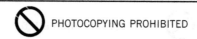

ISBN: 9780170229845

Other Transactions affecting Inventory

On occasions, the business owner may withdraw inventory from the business for personal use. The cost of these items must be removed from the business accounts. The GST which was claimed from Inland Revenue when the goods were purchased must also be repaid, because the goods no longer represent a business purchase.

> **Note**
>
> Writing down inventory to its estimated selling price is known as the *lower of cost and realisable value* rule.

Sometimes the selling price of inventory may be less than its cost. This could happen if the goods are out-of-date or damaged, or if it is necessary to reduce the selling price due to competition or lack of demand. In this event, the future economic benefit of the inventory is less than its carrying amount, so it is written down to the expected selling price. If the inventory were stated at historical cost under these circumstances, the amount shown would not be reliable since it would not represent the future economic benefit (cash to be received) to the business. The total assets (and hence the equity and profit) would be overstated. It may be difficult to estimate the selling price exactly, but this is a case where the accountant must exercise his or her judgement.

The above events do not appear in the special journals, so are recorded in the **general journal** and are posted from there to the ledger.

Consider the following example:

On 31 October, the following events occurred for *Kiri's Krafts:*

- Kiri took four felt kiwi home for her grandchildren. These had cost $15 each (excluding GST) and normally sell for $25 (including GST).
- Kiri discovered that a store nearby was selling woolly sheep for $15. These were very similar to the ones she had in stock, so she decided that she would need to reduce her selling price to match. There were eight in stock, which had cost $22 each (excluding GST).

Recording drawings

	A + Ex	=	L +	Eq + I
	Inventory control		GST payable	(Drawings)
Drawings, $69	– 60	=	+ 9 +	– 69
	Credit		Credit	Debit

> **Note**
>
> The selling price of the goods is not relevant because they have been taken by the owner and were not sold.

Ledger postings require the following entries:

Debit entries	$	Credit entries	$
Drawings	69	GST payable	9
		Inventory control	60
	$69		$69

The general journal entry appears as follows:

Kiri's Krafts
General Journal   Page 1

Date	Particulars	Ref	Dr $	Cr $
Oct 31	Drawings	520	69	
	GST payable	310		9
	Inventory control	130		60
	(for goods taken by owner for personal use)			

GST!

GST of $9 was claimed when these goods were purchased. This must be repaid to IRD later.

Writing down inventory

The woolly sheep on hand had cost $22 each (excluding GST) and had an estimated resale price of $15 each. This means that each item must be written down by $7. The total amount of the write-down = 8*$7 = $56.

Writing down inventory is an expense, since it represents the reduction in future economic benefit of an asset. The amount of the write-down is an estimate, because until the items are sold, there is no guarantee of the actual selling price.

	A	+	Ex	=	L	+	Eq	+	I
	Inventory control		**Inventory write-down**						
Inventory write-down, $56	– 56		+ 56						
	Credit		**Debit**						

Ledger postings require the following entries:

Debit entries	$	Credit entries	$
Inventory write-down	56	Inventory control	56

The general journal entry is:

Kiri's Krafts
General Journal — Page 1

Date	Particulars	Ref	Dr $	Cr $
Oct 31	Inventory write-down	730	56	
	Inventory control	130		56
	(for woolly sheep on hand written down to estimated net realisable value)			

NO GST!

GST was accounted for when the inventory was originally purchased.

The relevant ledger accounts after posting these entries are as follows:

Kiri's Krafts – General Ledger

Inventory control   130

Date	Particulars	Ref	$	Date	Particulars	Ref	$
Oct 1	Balance	b/d	1,945	Oct 31	Accounts payable	PRJ1	480
31	Accounts payable	PJ2	4,320		Cost of goods		
	Cost of goods				sold	SJ5	3,826
	sold	SRJ1	100		**Drawings**	GJ1	60
					Inventory		
					write-down	GJ1	56

GST payable   310

Date	Particulars	Ref	$	Date	Particulars	Ref	$
Oct 31	Accounts payable	PJ2	648	Oct 1	Balance	b/d	900
	Accounts	SRJ1	24	31	Accounts payable	PRJ1	72
	receivable				Accounts		
					receivable	SJ5	888
					Drawings	GJ1	9

Drawings   520

Date	Particulars	Ref	$	Date	Particulars	Ref	$
Oct 31	Inventory & GST	GJ1	69				

Inventory write-down   730

Date	Particulars	Ref	$	Date	Particulars	Ref	$
Oct 31	Inventory	GJ1	56				

Accounting – A Next Step PHOTOCOPYING PROHIBITED ISBN: 9780170229845

Activities

1 The documents below represent some of the transactions and other events of *Pampered Pets* for the month of February 2017. The business is registered for GST on the invoice basis.

TAX INVOICE	No: 1025
	4 February 2017

Petfood Supplies
INVOICE
GST No: 84-957-582

TO: Pampered Pets

FOR:	10 Cat food	$230.00
Total (incl GST)		$230.00

TAX INVOICE	No: 2257
	7 February 2017

Bird Breeders
INVOICE
GST No: 24-418-912

TO: Pampered Pets

FOR:	20 Budgies	$460.00
	4 Parrots	920.00
Total (incl GST)		$1,380.00

TAX INVOICE	No: 240
	14 February 2017

TOYS 4 PETS
INVOICE
GST No: 46-810-231

TO: Pampered Pets

FOR:	25 Dog toys	$414.00
	30 Cat toys	391.00
Total (incl GST)		$805.00

TAX INVOICE	No: 1096
	18 February 2017

Petfood Supplies
INVOICE
GST No: 84-957-582

TO: Pampered Pets

FOR:	100 Dog food	$920.00
	80 Bird seed	230.00
Total (incl GST)		$1,150.00

TAX INVOICE	No: 265
	25 February 2017

TOYS 4 PETS
INVOICE
GST No: 46-810-231

TO: Pampered Pets

FOR:	120 Bird toys	$690.00
	20 Cat toys	115.00
Total (incl GST)		$805.00

TAX INVOICE	No: 2284
	27 February 2017

Bird Breeders
INVOICE
GST No: 24-418-912

TO: Pampered Pets

FOR:	10 Canaries	$460.00
	15 Finches	920.00
Total (incl GST)		$1,380.00

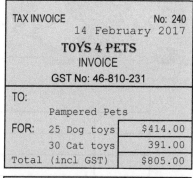

TAX INVOICE	No: 167
Inv Ref: 2257	8 Feb 2017

Bird Breeders
CREDIT NOTE
GST No: 24-418-912

TO: Pampered Pets

FOR:	2 cat food	
Total (incl GST)		$46.00

TAX INVOICE	No: 138
Inv Ref: 1096	22 Feb 2017

Petfood Supplies
CREDIT NOTE
GST No: 84-957-582

TO: Pampered Pets

FOR:	8 Bird seed	
Total (incl GST)		$23.00

TAX INVOICE	No: 629
Inv Ref: 265	28 Feb 2017

TOYS 4 PETS
CREDIT NOTE
GST No: 46-810-231

TO: Pampered Pets

FOR:	40 Bird toys	
Total (incl GST)		$230.00

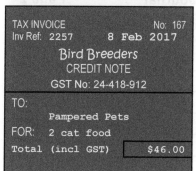

TAX INVOICE	No: 4687
	28 February 2017

Shop Outfitters Ltd
INVOICE
GST No: 14-877-932

TO: Pampered Pets

FOR:	Shelving	$1,400.00
	GST (15%)	210.00
Total (incl GST)		$1,610.00

MEMORANDUM

Pampered Pets

DATE: *10 February 2017*

Owner took home dog food costing $20 (excluding GST).

MEMORANDUM

Pampered Pets

DATE: *28 February 2017*

Cat food past use by date. Cost $60, probably can sell for half price.

Additional information:
- The sales journal (page 9) showed that cost of goods sold for the period was $4,280.
- Ledger balances at 1 February were:

Inventory	$5,420	Dr	Accounts payable	$4,750	Cr
Drawings	20,800	Dr	GST payable	$1,140	Cr
Cost of goods sold	43,600	Dr.			

DO THIS!

a Complete the purchases and purchases returns and allowances journals of *Pampered Pets* below.

b Prepare general journal entries to record the events described in the two memoranda.

c Post the journals to the ledger accounts provided. Balance the *inventory* account only. (The chart of accounts references are given on the accounts.)

Pampered Pets

Purchases Journal   Page 7

		Inv no	Ref	Total $	Inventory $	GST payable $

Purchases Returns and Allowances Journal   Page 2

		C/N no	Ref	Total $	Inventory $	GST payable $

General Journal   Page 3

Date	Particulars	Ref	Dr $	Cr $

 PHOTOCOPYING PROHIBITED

ISBN: 9780170229845

20

Pampered Pets
General Ledger

Inventory control   130

GST payable   310

Accounts payable   320

Drawings   520

Cost of goods sold   710

Inventory write-down   750

Internal Control over Accounts Payable

The main purposes of internal control over accounts payable are:

- to ensure that all goods purchased are for legitimate business purposes only
- to ensure that only goods that have been ordered are received and that only goods that have been received are paid for
- to ensure that the most competitive prices are paid for inventory
- to ensure that credits are received for returns to suppliers.

Document Flowcharts

The document flowchart below represents one system of accounting for credit purchases. This flowchart has been greatly simplified. Genuine document flowcharts show a good deal more detail than the one given. However, the flowchart is useful to show the movement of documents in the subsystem and the points where internal controls are applied.

Accounting – A Next Step
Accounts Payable Subsystem

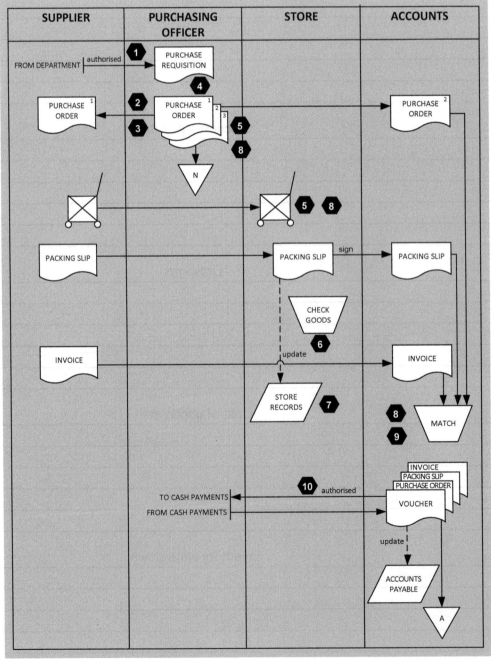

ISBN: 9780170229845

Guide to reading flowcharts

- The following symbols in the flowchart have special meanings:

| Document | Accounting Record | Process | File (Numerical Order) |

- The flowchart is divided into separate departments. There is a separate column for each of: supplier, store, purchasing and accounts payable. Each column represents a separation, or different people involved in the purchasing process.
- The flowchart shows the earliest events at the top, with later events following in sequence down the page.
- The document is reproduced as it flows from one department to the next.
- The flowchart is prepared from the business point of view. Thus, all business documents are filed but filing for the supplier is not shown.

Note

The **N** inside the file symbol means *filed in numerical order.*

An **A** inside the symbol means *filed in alphabetical order.*

The document flow for a manual accounts payable subsystem is as follows:

- The purchasing officer completes the **purchase order**. Two carbon copies are prepared.

- The top copy of the purchase order is *sent* to the supplier. Copy 2 is *sent* to the accounts clerk to await the arrival of the invoice. Copy 3 remains in numerical order in the invoice book.

- When the goods arrive, the packing slip is *checked* against the goods. The store **stock records** are *updated* and the packing slip is *signed* and *sent* to the accounts clerk. (If the goods listed on the packing slip are not physically present, this fact is noted on the packing slip.) In some firms, the store staff who unpack the goods prepare a separate **receiving report** rather than mark items off against the packing slip. A different member of the store staff then checks this receiving report against the packing slip. This system provides an additional check that the quantity and description of goods received are correct.

- The invoice from the supplier is sent directly to the accounts clerk. The accounts clerks *matches* three documents: the **purchase order**, **packing slip** and **invoice** and *checks* that all details of goods ordered, received and invoiced are correct and that calculations are accurate.

- The accounts clerk prepares a **payment voucher** and attaches this to the other three documents to form a **voucher set**. The voucher set is *sent* to a senior member of staff who has the authority to approve payments.

- When payment has been approved, the documents enter the cash payments subsystem. When payment has been made, the voucher sets are *filed* alphabetically (by name of supplier) in the accounts department.

Note

A *purchase requisition* is a document that authorises the purchasing officer to order goods on behalf of a particular person or department.

In larger businesses, with many departments, a **purchase requisition** is completed within the department that is requesting the goods. This requisition is approved by a senior member of that department before being forwarded to the purchasing department. This helps to ensure that purchases are properly authorised and are for legitimate business purposes. It also enables managers to keep control over their budgets.

Internal Control

Simple procedures together with the correct separation of duties can ensure that internal control is adequate. The position of each of the required internal controls is shown on the flowchart, and described below, together with its purpose.

Internal Control	Description	Purpose
1	Purchase requisition authorised by senior staff in department requesting order	Ensures goods ordered have been approved and are for legitimate business purposes
2	Prices confirmed with supplier before order sent	Ensures price to be paid for goods is known in advance. Assists in obtaining best possible price.
3	Purchase order forms pre-numbered	Prevents issue of false documents and removal of copies. Enables matching of order with invoice from supplier (which will quote order number).
4	Purchase order double-checked against purchase requisition before order sent	Prevents firm having to pay for incorrectly ordered goods that may not be able to be returned
5	Person placing order different from person checking inwards goods	Prevents goods being ordered for private purposes and intercepted when they are delivered
6	Inwards goods checked against packing slip	Ensures that goods invoiced were actually received
7	Store records updated when goods received	Maintains accurate records of inventory on hand that can be checked against stock counts to maintain control over inventory
8	Person checking and approving the invoice should not have ordered the goods and should not have taken delivery of them	Ensures that correct prices are paid to suppliers and that order for goods is a legitimate business order
9	Details on purchase order, packing slip and invoice matched before payment voucher is prepared	Ensures that goods that were invoiced were both ordered and received before invoice is sent to be paid
10	Voucher set approved for payment by senior member of staff	Ensures that invoices paid are for legitimate business purposes.

There are further internal controls relating to accounts payable that have been covered in previous sections, but are not shown in detail on the flowchart. These relate to the payment of cash to suppliers:

Description	Purpose
Separation of approval of cash payments from ordering and receiving goods	Ensured goods cannot be ordered for personal use and approved for payment by the business
Person authorising cash payment not the same person making the payment	Prevents theft of cash from business bank account
Separation of recording cash payments from updating accounts payable records	Prevents diversion of payments from supplier accounts to another account and showing supplier account has been paid when it has not.

ISBN: 9780170229845

Activities

1 Describe internal controls that could be introduced to prevent the following events from taking place:

a the payment of an invoice for goods that had not been received

_____

_____

_____

_____

_____

b i a purchasing officer ordered goods for personal use

_____

_____

_____

_____

_____

ii the purchasing officer intercepted the goods when they were delivered to the office

_____

_____

_____

_____

_____

c a supplier's invoice was paid even though it overcharged for the goods received

_____

_____

_____

_____

_____

d a supplier sent goods that had not been ordered and then sent an invoice for them which was paid

_____

_____

_____

_____

e a supplier invoiced a firm for twice as many goods as had been supplied and the invoice was paid.

_____

_____

_____

_____

2 Joe Bloggs owns and operates a small clothing store in a suburban shopping mall. He has two staff working for him and the shop is open seven days a week. Due to family commitments, Joe is unable to be at the shop all the time. He has come to rely upon his staff to help run the business. The store operates as follows:

- When anyone notices that stock of a particular item is running low, that person writes a purchase order on the computer, using the firm's letterhead logo and emails it to the supplier, at the same time phoning the order through.
- When the goods arrive, whoever has time and is working that day unpacks them and checks them against the packing slip. If everything is correct, he or she then puts the goods out on the shelves and throws the packing slip away. If there is a problem with the order, the supplier is contacted and the goods are left for Joe to sort out next time he is in.
- When the invoices arrive, Joe pays them straight away because he is afraid he will forget to do them otherwise. He pays by internet banking and prints out the transaction record which he then staples to the invoice and files away in date order so that he can reconcile his bank statement later on.

DO THIS!

a List the problems that Joe might experience as the result of using this system.

b Describe an alternative system which you suggest will prevent these problems from arising in future. Joe cannot afford to employ any more staff.

a List the problems that Joe might experience as the result of using this system.

_____
_____
_____
_____
_____
_____
_____
_____
_____
_____

b Describe an alternative system which you suggest will prevent these problems from arising in future. Joe cannot afford to employ any more staff.

_____
_____
_____
_____
_____
_____
_____
_____
_____
_____
_____
_____
_____
_____
_____

_____

_____

_____

_____

_____

_____

_____

_____

_____

3 The following is a description of the process used by *Efficient Manufacturing Limited* to purchase raw materials:

- When supplies reach their re-order point, the charge storeperson emails a *purchase requisition form* to the **purchasing department**.
- The purchasing officer prepares a *purchase order* and emails it to the **supplier**. A copy is sent to the **raw materials clerk** who files it in the outstanding orders file on her computer. The purchase order is automatically numbered by the computer software.
- When the goods arrive, the *packing slip* is checked against the goods and, if correct, signed by the storeperson who unpacks them. The storeperson updates the store records and sends the packing slip to the raw materials clerk who transfers the purchase order to the **RECEIVED** folder on her computer. She then updates the master inventory records on her computer and files the packing slip in a temporary file for the accounts clerk to retrieve later.
- When the *invoice* arrives, it is sent straight to the **accounts** department. The accounts clerk accesses the purchase order from the **RECEIVED** file on the computer system and retrieves the packing slip from the raw materials clerk. She matches the three documents and if everything is correct, she prepares a *voucher* and processes the payment using the firm's online banking system. She then files the voucher set **alphabetically** by supplier, in date order.

DO THIS!

Answer the questions below relating to the purchases subsystem of *Efficient Manufacturing Limited.*

a Explain the purpose of a purchase requisition form.

_____

_____

_____

_____

_____

_____

_____

b Explain why purchase orders for *Efficient Manufacturing Limited* should be pre-numbered.

_____

_____

_____

_____

_____

_____

_____

_____

c Explain how checking the packing slip against the goods received helps to safeguard the business assets of *Efficient Manufacturing Limited.*

_____

_____

_____

_____

_____

_____

d Explain why the invoice from the supplier is sent directly to the accounts department of *Efficient Manufacturing Limited* and not to the purchasing officer.

_____

_____

_____

_____

_____

_____

_____

e As well as updating the inventory records from packing slips received by the store, the raw materials clerk uses other factory documents to update the same inventory records with details of raw materials that are issued to the factory for use in production.

i Suggest a reason why the **store** of *Efficient Manufacturing Limited* maintains one set of inventory records and the **raw materials clerk** maintains another, separate set.

_____

_____

_____

_____

_____

ii Suggest how *Efficient Manufacturing Limited* could establish the correct quantities of inventories on hand if the two sets of inventory records show differences.

_____

_____

_____

_____

iii List reasons why the two sets of inventory records might be different.

_____

_____

_____

_____

_____

ISBN: 9780170229845

f Explain why the voucher set is filed **both** alphabetically by supplier **and** in date order after the payment has been processed.

_____

_____

_____

_____

_____

_____

_____

_____

_____

g i Identify and describe one serious internal control weakness in the purchases subsystem.

_____

_____

_____

_____

_____

ii Explain how the internal control weakness you have identified above could place the assets of _Efficient Manufacturing Limited_ at risk.

_____

_____

_____

_____

_____

iii Suggest how _Efficient Manufacturing Limited_ could overcome this internal control weakness. The business cannot afford to employ any more staff.

_____

_____

_____

_____

_____

_____

_____

_____

_____

_____

_____

Inventory Recording and Measurement

This chapter has been concerned with the recording and processing of transactions related to the purchase of inventory. However, the purchase of inventory is only the first step in the operating cycle of the firm. The cycle ends when the inventory has been sold and the customers have paid cash.

In between the time when the inventory is purchased and when it is sold, the inventory remains in the business. During this phase, internal control and security are very important. At the end of the reporting period, the measurement of inventory on hand is critical in determining the final amounts for both profit and current assets of the business.

Events relating to inventory are represented in the following diagram:

Recording Inventory

In previous courses we used the **periodic inventory system** to record inventory. This name is derived from the way the system operates: at the end of the reporting period (or whenever financial statements are required) the firm must carry out a stocktake to ascertain the physical quantities of goods on hand. This is necessary because no records of stock movements are kept during the reporting period. The calculation of the cost of goods sold thus becomes a periodic exercise – it cannot be done without a stocktake which, for most firms, is too expensive a process to be done on a daily or weekly basis.

When the periodic system is used to record inventory, the cost of goods sold for the period is calculated as shown in the following trading statement:

<table>
<tr><td colspan="3" align="center">**Easy Electronics**</td></tr>
<tr><td colspan="3" align="center">**Trading Statement for the year ended 30 June 2018**</td></tr>
<tr><td></td><td align="center">$</td><td align="center">$</td></tr>
<tr><td>**Revenue**</td><td></td><td></td></tr>
<tr><td>Sales</td><td></td><td>248,000</td></tr>
<tr><td>*Less:* Sales returns</td><td></td><td>(3,500)</td></tr>
<tr><td>Net sales</td><td></td><td>244,500</td></tr>
<tr><td>*Less: Cost of goods sold*</td><td></td><td></td></tr>
<tr><td>Inventory, beginning of year</td><td>23,000</td><td></td></tr>
<tr><td>*Plus:* Purchases</td><td>85,700</td><td></td></tr>
<tr><td>*Less:* Purchases returns</td><td>(1,400)</td><td></td></tr>
<tr><td>Cost of goods available for sale</td><td>107,300</td><td></td></tr>
<tr><td>*Less:* Inventory, end of year</td><td>(21,700)</td><td></td></tr>
<tr><td>Cost of goods sold</td><td></td><td>85,600</td></tr>
<tr><td>Gross profit</td><td></td><td>$158,900</td></tr>
</table>

Remember!

The cost of sales includes:

- cost of goods sold

- any other expenses which are incurred in getting the goods into the location and condition where they can be sold.

Accounting – A Next Step

ISBN: 9780170229845

Important!

- Sales returns have been deducted from the gross sales in the trading statement.

- Purchases returns have been deducted from purchases to produce a figure for net purchases in the cost of goods sold section.

- This is a simplified example. Other expenses such as customs duty and packaging costs are added to the cost of goods sold to calculate the cost of sales.

Remember!

Gross profit = Sales – Cost of sales

Cost of sales = Cost of goods sold + other trading expenses

The stocktaking process provides details of the quantities of goods on hand at the end of the reporting period. However, in order to prepare the financial statements, it is necessary to assign a **dollar** amount to inventory.

Why is Measurement of Inventory Important?

The dollar amount of inventory affects the profit for the period through the calculation of cost of goods sold and it also affects the current assets total in the statement of financial position. Hence, several key ratios and percentages are also affected by inventory measurement. These are:
- Gross and net profit percentages
- Working capital and current ratio
- Markup percentage
- Equity ratio
- Rate of inventory turnover.

We will examine these ratios in more detail later in the course. However, since financial statements and ratios/percentages are affected by the measurement of inventory, it follows that this measurement is very important in determining what information is provided to users for their decision-making.

Measuring the Inventory

Once the physical quantities have been established, there are several approaches that can be taken to assigning a value to inventory. In New Zealand there are three that are commonly used.

When inventory items are clearly distinguishable from each other, for example the vehicles in a used car yard, then the **actual cost** method is used. This means that the inventory is measured at the price which was paid for it. However, when a business has stocks that consist of large quantities of similar items that are not able to be distinguished from each other (for example, stocks of baked beans in a supermarket), there are two options available:

First In First Out (FIFO), which *assumes* that the first inventory purchased during the year is the first to be sold. Under this assumption, the measurement of the closing inventory will be the *most recent* prices paid.

Weighted Average Cost (WAC), which measures the inventory at the average per item price paid for both opening inventory and purchases made during the year.

Consider the following example:

A firm had 100 widgets in stock at the beginning of the year which had cost $40 each. The following purchases were made during the year:

Quantity	Price	Total cost
200	$40	$8,000
300	45	13,500
100	60	6,000
600		**$27,500**

At the end of the year, 150 widgets were on hand.

First-in first-out (FIFO) method

We assume that the 150 widgets remaining were from the *most recent* purchases. This means that the closing inventory of 150 units will consist of the last batch of 100 purchased at $60 each and 50 of the previous batch which had cost $45 each.

The total of **closing inventory** is thus:

$$
\begin{aligned}
\text{Closing inventory} &= (100 * \$60) + (50 * \$45) \\
&= \$6,000 + 2,250 \\
&= \$8,250
\end{aligned}
$$

The amount shown for closing inventory in the financial statements is $8,250.

$$
\begin{aligned}
\text{Cost of goods sold} &= \text{opening inventory} + \text{purchases} - \text{closing inventory} \\
&= [100 * \$40] + \$27,500 - \$8,250 \\
&= \$23,250
\end{aligned}
$$

Note that all goods are accounted for: at the end of the reporting period the opening inventory and new goods purchased will either have been sold or remain on hand.

	Quantity	Total cost			Quantity	Total cost
Opening	100	$ 4,000		COGS	550	$23,250
Purchases	600	27,500	**=**	Closing	150	8,250
	700	**$31,500**			**700**	**$31,500**

Weighted average cost (WAC) method

This method states the closing inventory at the *average price* per item paid during the year. If we reconsider the example given above using the weighted average cost method, we have the following:

	Quantity	Price	Total cost
Opening inventory	100	$40	$4,000
Purchase	200	40	8,000
Purchase	300	45	13,500
Purchase	100	60	6,000
Total	**700**		**$31,500**

The weighted average cost of these items is the total cost divided by the total number of items:

$$
\begin{aligned}
\text{Weighted average cost} &= \frac{\$31,500}{700} \\
&= \$45
\end{aligned}
$$

PHOTOCOPYING PROHIBITED

ISBN: 9780170229845

The total of the closing inventory is thus 150 units at $45 each:

Closing inventory   =   150*$45

                                    = $6,750

The amount shown for closing inventory in the financial statements is $6,750.

Cost of goods sold   =   opening inventory + purchases − closing inventory

                            =   [100*$40] + $27,500 − $6,750

                            = $24,750

Once again, all goods are accounted for; at the end of the reporting period the opening inventory and new goods purchased will either have been sold or remain on hand. However, since the closing inventory is $1,500 less under the WAC measurement assumption when compared to the FIFO assumption ($8,250 − 6,750), the cost of goods sold is higher by the same amount.

	Quantity	Total cost				Quantity	Total cost
Opening	100	$ 4,000			COGS	550	$24,750
Purchases	600	27,500	**=**		Closing	150	6,750
	700	**$31,500**				**700**	**$31,500**

The FIFO assumption gives a larger amount for closing inventory than the WAC assumption. This has occurred because each batch of purchases had cost more than the previous batch, since *prices paid for inventory rose throughout the year*. The most recent purchases are thus the most expensive and are *assumed* to be the goods remaining on hand at the end of the reporting period. FIFO gives a correspondingly lower amount for cost of goods sold. The difference in the reported amounts for closing inventory and cost of goods sold under the FIFO and WAC measurement assumptions depends on the trend in the cost of goods purchased throughout the year:

Trend in prices paid	Closing inventory	Cost of goods sold
Increasing	Higher using FIFO	Lower using FIFO
Decreasing	Higher using WAC	Lower using WAC
No change	No difference	No difference

It is important to remember that FIFO and WAC are **measurement assumptions** only. When there are large quantities of similar goods, the physical flow of goods may not actually be 'first-in first-out' even though that is the assumption used when the historical cost is measured. Similarly, no single item will usually cost exactly the same amount as the WAC figure. FIFO and WAC are simply **assumptions** that enable us to assign a dollar amount to closing inventory and, as a consequence, to cost of goods sold.

The need to assign such amounts to closing inventory arises because we must prepare financial statements on a *periodic* basis. When we use a periodic inventory system, closing inventory is regarded as a period-end adjustment to the purchases expense.

When we use the periodic system of recording inventory, the calculation of weighted average cost can be time-consuming, especially if a manual accounting system is being used and there are frequent purchases of inventory made throughout the year. When a periodic system is being used with a manual accounting system, the FIFO assumption is most commonly applied. Computerised systems tend to use weighted average cost.

The adjustment for closing inventory is a period-end adjustment that is carried out because we must measure assets at the end of the reporting period to prepare the statement of financial position. It is necessary to state inventory as accurately as possible so that the reported amounts for total assets and equity (and the reported profit for the period) are *faithfully represented*[1].

What about old inventory?

Sometimes the inventory on hand may become out-of-date or decline in popularity for some reason, such as clothing being old-fashioned, or equipment being replaced by more modern technology. It may be necessary to reduce the selling price to clear the inventory and obtain whatever cash is available from the market for the goods. In these cases the market value of the inventory may be less than the price that was paid for the goods when they were first purchased.

If the inventory were stated at historical cost under these circumstances, the amount shown would not *faithfully represent* the future economic benefit (cash to be received) to the business. The total assets (and hence equity and profit) would be overstated. It may be difficult to estimate the selling price exactly, but this is a case where the accountant must exercise his or her judgement and use the best information available.

The general rule applying to the measurement of inventory is[2]:

> **Inventories shall be measured at the lower of cost and net realisable value.**

Cost means historical cost, measured using either first-in first-out or weighted average cost.

Net realisable value means the cash that will be received for the inventory in the market, *less any costs incurred in selling the inventory*. These costs must relate to selling the particular inventory concerned. For example, if *extra* advertising expenses were necessary to clear old stock, the expected amount of these costs would be deducted from the amount shown for inventory in the statement of financial position. If the goods were to be sold by auction, expected commissions would be deducted.

The amount of any reduction in the carrying amount of inventory caused through stating it at net realisable value in the statement of financial position is an **expense**. It is often named *inventory write-down*. An inventory write-down is *material*[3] and must be shown as a *separate* expense in the income statement[4].

> ### Remember!
>
> - **Inventories are shown at historical cost unless the expected realisable value is less than historical cost.**
> - **Historical cost is determined by using *either* the FIFO or WAC measurement assumptions for inventory.**

---

1 **Faithful representation** is a qualitative characteristic of useful financial information. This characteristic is explained fully in the *Accounting Concepts* workbook of this series.
2 NZ IAS 2, paragraph 9
3 **Materiality** is an aspect of the **relevance** qualitative characteristic of useful financial information. This characteristic is explained fully in the *Accounting Concepts* workbook of this series.
4 NZ IAS 1, paragraph 98 (a)

 PHOTOCOPYING PROHIBITED

ISBN: 9780170229845

Activities

1 A retail firm selling plasma TV sets had an opening stock of 200 units that had cost $500 each (excluding GST) at 1 July 2017. In the year to 30 June 2018, the following purchases were made:

Quantity	Price (excluding GST)	Total cost (excluding GST)
100	$520	$52,000
200	550	110,000
100	560	56,000

At 30 June 2018, the firm had 250 units on hand.

DO THIS!

a If the average selling price of the TV sets was $1,000, calculate the total sales (excluding GST) for the year.

b Calculate the amount of closing inventory at 30 June 2018 under each of the following assumptions:
  i First-in first-out (FIFO)
  ii Weighted average cost (WAC).

c Complete the table provided to show the gross profit for the year under each of the above assumptions.

d Fully explain why the gross profit calculated using WAC is different from that calculated using FIFO.

a If the average selling price of the TV sets was $1,000, calculate the total sales (excluding GST) for the year.

ANSWER: Total sales = $ _____

b Calculate the amount of closing inventory at 30 June 2018 under each of the following assumptions:

  i First-in first-out

ANSWER: Closing inventory = $ _____

  ii Weighted average cost

ANSWER: Closing inventory = $ _____

c Complete the table below to show gross profit.

	i FIFO	ii WAC
Sales		
Less: **Cost of goods sold**		
Opening inventory		
Plus: Purchases		
Goods available for sale		
Less: Closing inventory		
Cost of goods sold		
Gross profit		

d Fully explain why the gross profit calculated using WAC is different from that calculated using FIFO.

_____

_____

_____

_____

_____

_____

_____

_____

_____

_____

2 Your friend Tamati has recently inherited a country general store from his grandfather. He decided to move back to the area and run the store himself. However, when he arrived, he found that his grandfather's accounting records had not been kept up-to-date. He knows that you study accounting and he has sent you an email asking for your help. Relevant extracts are as follows:

I have a copy of last year's accounts from the accountant but I don't think Grandad has done much in the way of book-keeping this past year. Luckily all his bank statements and chequebooks are here, but I am having a terrible time trying to figure out what to do about the stocktaking. HELP! Grandad didn't even own a computer, let alone use one in the business.

There's a stock figure in last year's accounts, but goodness knows how accurate that was. I think he might have made it up! The accountant said we have to do a set of financial statements before I take over the business. He's asked me to give him a figure for the stock on hand now. What's that all about?

I have counted up all the stock but I don't know how to work out what it's worth. All Grandad's invoices are here but prices have changed all the time so which ones do I use?

Also, there's a whole pile of old stock out the back. I reckon some if it's been there for 50 years or more. A guy down the road offered me $1,000 for the lot as long as I take it round, but I will need to hire a trailer and that will cost me $35.

DO THIS!

Answer the questions on the next page. Remember that Tamati knows very little about accounting.

ISBN: 9780170229845

a Explain **fully** the purpose of calculating a figure for closing inventory before preparing the financial statements.

_____

_____

_____

_____

_____

_____

_____

b Explain **to Tamati:**

i the general principle that applies to the measurement of inventory

_____

_____

_____

_____

_____

_____

_____

_____

_____

_____

ii how he should go about establishing a dollar amount for closing inventory to give to the accountant.

_____

_____

_____

_____

_____

_____

_____

_____

_____

_____

c Recommend an amount for the old inventory that Tamati has found out the back and explain your reasoning. (Ignore GST.)

_____

_____

_____

_____

_____

_____

Inventory Subsidiary Ledger

A subsidiary ledger is a separate ledger that is outside the main, general ledger of the firm. A subsidiary ledger contains separate accounts for individual items, the total of which is shown in a **control account** in the general ledger. The *accounts receivable subsidiary ledger* is covered in the *Accounts Receivable* module of this course. The accounts receivable subsidiary ledger contains a separate account for each debtor and the totals are recorded in the *accounts receivable control* account in the general ledger.

It is possible to use a subsidiary ledger for *any* asset or liability accounts. Most firms operate an *accounts payable subsidiary ledger* to keep records of dealings with individual creditors. This operates in exactly the same way as for accounts receivable, with an *accounts payable control* account in the general ledger that represents the totals of all transactions with creditors.

If records are kept for individual inventory items, an **inventory subsidiary ledger** can be used. Once again there is a control account in the general ledger. The **inventory control** account represents the totals of transactions relating to inventory.

A subsidiary ledger can only be used for inventory if the business uses a **perpetual inventory system** to record its inventory transactions, because details of all movements of individual inventory items are required to prepare it.

The Perpetual Inventory System

The basic difference between the perpetual inventory system and the periodic system is that the perpetual system maintains a record of inventory movements throughout the reporting period. This means that every time a purchase or sale is made, a record of the goods transferred is also made. Thus, at any time, a **theoretical record** of the goods on hand is available. Since records are kept of all goods sold, it is possible to calculate the gross profit without carrying out a stocktake because the cost of goods sold is known at all times. If the *periodic* system is used, there is no theoretical record of inventory. The only way the gross profit can be calculated is to carry out a physical stocktake. Under this system, it is not possible to tell whether any stock is missing or not.

Recording transactions for individual stock items is normally carried out on an **inventory card** which looks similar to a 3-column ledger account. The way the card is completed depends on which *measurement assumption* (FIFO or WAC) is used.

> **Note**
>
> The inventory ledger is a theoretical record because it shows the quantity of inventory that *should* be on hand. This can only be confirmed by a physical stocktake.

Consider the following example:

The table below shows the inventory purchases and (purchases returns) made by *Kiri's Krafts* in October. (All amounts exclude GST.)

Date	Supplier	Paua pendant	Kete	Woolly sheep	Felt kiwi	Table mat	Paua earrings
Oct 2	Colinette's Crafts			20 @ $20	40 @ $15		
4	Flaxworks		10 @ $90				
4	Colinette's Crafts			(8 @ $20)			
14	Jill's Jewellery	10 @ $30					10 @ $40
16	Jill's Jewellery						(2 @ $40)
20	Colinette's Crafts			10 @ $22	20 @ $15		
21	Flaxworks		4 @ $100			32 @ $20	
24	Flaxworks					(12 @ $20)	
30	Jill's Jewellery						4 @ $40

The purchases and purchases returns and allowances journals for the month are shown on the next page.

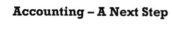

 PHOTOCOPYING PROHIBITED

ISBN: 9780170229845

Kiri's Krafts
Purchases Journal — Page 2

Date		Particulars	Invoice No	Ref	Total $	Inventory $	GST $
Oct	2	Colinette's Crafts	566		1,150	1,000	150
	4	Flaxworks	215		1,035	900	135
	14	Jill's Jewellery	356		805	700	105
	20	Colinette's Crafts	572		598	520	78
	21	Flaxworks	220		1,196	1,040	156
	30	Jill's Jewellery	371		184	160	24
					$4,968	$4,320	$648
					320	130	310

Purchases Returns and Allowances Journal — Page 1

Date		Particulars	Credit Note No	Ref	Total $	Inventory $	GST $
Oct	4	Colinette's Crafts	254		184	160	24
	16	Jill's Jewellery	442		92	80	12
	24	Flaxworks	899		276	240	36
					$552	$480	$72
					320	130	310

Quantities of goods sold and (returned) during the month are shown below.

Date		Customer	Paua pendant	Kete	Woolly sheep	Felt kiwi	Table mat	Paua earrings
Oct	3	Kerikeri Store		6				
	15	Rotorua Souvenirs			10			
	19	Te Anau Travel	12	4		25	20	5
	22	Te Anau Travel	(2)					
	25	Te Anau Travel			8			
	27	Rotorua Souvenirs				20		3
	29	Rotorua Souvenirs						(1)
	31	Kerikeri Store		10			4	

The sales and sales returns and allowances journals are shown below.

Kiri's Krafts
Sales Journal — Page 5

Date		Particulars	Invoice No	Ref	Total $	Sales $	GST $
Oct	3	Kerikeri Store	210		966	840	126
	15	Rotorua Souvenirs	211		345	300	45
	19	Te Anau Travel	212		2,829	2,460	369
	25	Te Anau Travel	213		276	240	36
	27	Rotorua Souvenirs	214		667	580	87
	31	Kerikeri Store	215		1,725	1,500	225
					$6,808	$5,920	$888
					120	610	310

	Kiri's Krafts Sales Returns and Allowances Journal					Page 1
Date	Particulars	Credit Note No	Ref	Total $	Sales returns $	GST $
Oct 22	Te Anau Travel	013		115	100	15
29	Rotorua Souvenirs	014		69	60	9
				$184	$160	$24
				120	611	310

The following events occurred on 31 October:
- Kiri took four felt kiwi home as gifts for her grandchildren.
- During the end-of-month stocktake on 31 October, Kiri discovered that she had accidentally recorded the paua *pendants* purchased the previous day from *Jill's Jewellery* on the inventory card for paua *earrings*.
- The stocktake also revealed that one tablemat was missing.
- Kiri discovered that a store nearby was selling woolly sheep for $15 plus GST. These were very similar to the ones she had in stock, so she decided that she would need to reduce her selling price to match.

First-in first-out

The inventory card for paua pendants prepared on the first-in first-out basis is shown below.

INVENTORY RECORD CARD

Product: Paua Pendant **Code No:** 0129

Description: Leather strap **Reorder Point:** 5

Supplier: Jill's Jewellery **Reorder Quantity:** 10

DATE	PARTICULARS	IN			OUT			BALANCE		
		Quantity	Cost per unit	Total	Quantity	Cost per unit	Total	Quantity	Cost per unit	Total
Oct 1	Balance							5	25	125
14	Purchases – Jill's Jewellery	10	30	300				10	30	300
19	Sales – Te Anau Travel				5	25	125			
					7	30	210	3	30	90
22	Returns – Te Anau Travel	2	30	60				5	30	150
31	Purchases – Jill's Jewellery	4	40	160				4	40	160

Important!

- The stock item has a number: 0129. This enables the item to be distinguished from other items.

- The card shows the name of the usual supplier and the **reorder quantity**. This is the normal quantity of goods purchased in a single order. If you examine the transactions, you will see that the reorder quantity is ten units and that ten units were purchased on 14 October. On 31 October only four units were purchased. Maybe the supplier did not have sufficient stock on hand to supply the normal quantity.

 PHOTOCOPYING PROHIBITED

ISBN: 9780170229845

Important!

- The **reorder point** is also shown. This is the level of stock at which more must be ordered to maintain a continuous supply to customers. In this case, the reorder point is five units. As soon as the stock level reaches this point a new order is placed.

- The cost of inventory is recorded separately for each batch of purchases. For example, after the purchase had been made on 14 October, the balance column showed two groups – the opening balance of five units at $25 each and the new purchase of ten units at $30 each.

- When a sale is made, the oldest inventory is assumed to be sold first. On 19 October, 12 units were sold. This consists of the opening five units plus seven of the units purchased on 14 October. The closing balance becomes the remaining three units from the purchase on 14 October.

- The entry on 31 October is a transfer from the inventory card for paua earrings. Kiri had accidentally recorded this on the wrong card in the first instance.

The inventory card for kete is shown below.

INVENTORY RECORD CARD

Product:	Kete	Code No:	0133
Description:	Medium	Reorder Point:	5
Supplier:	Flaxworks	Reorder Quantity:	as available

DATE	PARTICULARS	IN			OUT			BALANCE		
		Quantity	Cost per unit	Total	Quantity	Cost per unit	Total	Quantity	Cost per unit	Total
Oct 1	Balance							8	90	720
3	Sales – Kerikeri Store				6	90	540	2	90	180
4	Purchases – Flaxworks	10	90	900				12	90	1,080
19	Sales – Te Anau Travel				4	90	360	8	90	720
21	Purchases – Flaxworks	4	100	400				4	100	400
31	Sales – Kerikeri Store				8	90	720			
					2	100	200	2	100	200

Important!

- The purchase price on 4 October was the same as for the opening stock. Thus the balance column requires only a single line after this purchase because all items had cost the same amount.

- The sale on 31 October consisted of ten units. Eight of these were from the purchase on 4 October at $90 each and the remaining two were from the purchase on 21 October at $100 each.

ISBN: 9780170229845

Inventory cards for the other four items of inventory are shown below.

INVENTORY RECORD CARD

Product:	Woolly sheep	Code No:	0142
Description:	10 cm	Reorder Point:	10
Supplier:	Colinette's Crafts	Reorder Quantity:	20

DATE	PARTICULARS	IN			OUT			BALANCE		
		Quantity	Cost per unit	Total	Quantity	Cost per unit	Total	Quantity	Cost per unit	Total
Oct 1	Balance							4	20	80
2	Purchases – Colinette's Crafts	20	20	400				24	20	480
4	Returns – Colinette's Crafts				8	20	160	16	20	320
15	Sales – Rotorua Souvenirs				10	20	200	6	20	120
20	Purchases – Colinette's Crafts	10	22	220				10	22	220
25	Sales – Te Anau Travel				6	20	120			
					2	22	44	8	22	176
31	**Write-down**				8	7	56	8	15	120

Important!

- The woolly sheep on hand at the end of the month are written down to the lower of cost and net realisable value. They had cost $22 each, but due to the fact that a local competitor was selling them for $15, Kiri had decided to sell them for the same price. This represents a reduction in the carrying amount of $7 per unit.

INVENTORY RECORD CARD

Product:	Felt kiwi	Code No:	0145
Description:	Miniature	Reorder Point:	30
Supplier:	Colinette's Crafts	Reorder Quantity:	20

DATE	PARTICULARS	IN			OUT			BALANCE		
		Quantity	Cost per unit	Total	Quantity	Cost per unit	Total	Quantity	Cost per unit	Total
Oct 1	Balance							30	12	360
2	Purchases – Colinette's Crafts	40	15	600				40	15	600
19	Sales – Te Anau Travel				25	12	300	5	12	60
								40	15	600
20	Purchases – Colinette's Crafts	20	15	300				5	12	60
								60	15	900
27	Sales – Rotorua Souvenirs				5	12	60			
					15	15	225	45	15	675
31	**Drawings – Kiri**				4	15	60	41	15	615

Important!

- Kiri took four felt kiwi home for her grandchildren on 31 October. These are shown in the **OUT** columns of the inventory card.

 PHOTOCOPYING PROHIBITED

ISBN: 9780170229845

INVENTORY RECORD CARD

Product: *Tablemat* Code No: *0152*
Description: *45 x 30* Reorder Point: *12*
Supplier: *Flaxworks* Reorder Quantity: *as available*

DATE	PARTICULARS	IN			OUT			BALANCE		
		Quantity	Cost per unit	Total	Quantity	Cost per unit	Total	Quantity	Cost per unit	Total
Oct 1	Balance							25	18	450
19	Sales – Te Anau Travel				20	18	360	5	18	90
21	Purchases – Flaxworks	32	20	640				5	18	90
								32	20	640
24	Returns – Flaxworks				12	20	240	5	18	90
								20	20	400
31	Sales – Kerikeri Store				4	18	72	1	18	18
								20	20	400
	Inventory shortage				1	18	18	20	20	400

Important!

- On 31 October Kiri carried out a stocktake and found only 20 tablemats on hand. The missing tablemat is recorded as an **inventory shortage**.

INVENTORY RECORD CARD

Product: *Paua earrings* Code No: *0160*
Description: *Assorted shapes* Reorder Point: *6*
Supplier: *Jill's Jewellery* Reorder Quantity: *as available*

DATE	PARTICULARS	IN			OUT			BALANCE		
		Quantity	Cost per unit	Total	Quantity	Cost per unit	Total	Quantity	Cost per unit	Total
Oct 1	Balance							6	35	210
14	Purchases – Jill's Jewellery	10	40	400				10	40	400
16	Returns – Jill's Jewellery				2	40	80	6	35	210
								8	40	320
19	Sales – Te Anau Travel				5	35	175	1	35	35
								8	40	320
27	Sales – Rotorua Souvenirs				1	35	35			
					2	40	80	6	40	240
29	Returns – Rotorua Souvenirs	1	40	40				7	40	280
30	Purchases – Jill's Jewellery	4	40	160				11	40	440
31	**Error – Jill's Jewellery**				4	40	160	7	40	280

Important!

- On 30 October Kiri accidentally recorded the purchase of paua pendants on the card for paua earrings. She corrected this on 31 October.

ISBN: 9780170229845

 PHOTOCOPYING PROHIBITED

Inventory Subsystem

Activities

1 *Albany TV* uses a perpetual inventory system to record the sale and purchase of major home appliances. The following transactions relate to one model of microwave oven for the month of June 2018. Amounts included GST unless otherwise stated.

Jun	1	Balance on hand, 5 units @ $160 each (excluding GST)
	5	Sold 3 units for $322 each on credit
	12	Purchased 5 units @ $180 (excluding GST) each on credit
	14	Returned one faulty unit from the opening stock to the supplier
	20	Sold 4 units for $322 each on credit
	29	Owner took one unit home for personal use.

DO THIS!

a Prepare the inventory record card, using the first-in first-out basis, to record the transactions above.

b Prepare journal entries (using *general* journal format, without narrations) to record the transactions that occurred on the following dates:
  i June 5
  ii June 14
  iii June 29.

c Calculate the cost of microwave ovens sold during June.

a Prepare the inventory record card, using the first-in first-out basis, to record the transactions above. (You should use the terms **sale**, **purchase**, **returns** or other appropriate description in the PARTICULARS column.)

INVENTORY RECORD CARD

Product:	*Microwave*	Code No:	*24687*
Description:	*Basic 40L*	Reorder Point:	*2*
Supplier:	*Homelex*	Reorder Quantity:	*5*

DATE	PARTICULARS	IN			OUT			BALANCE		
		Quantity	Cost per unit	Total	Quantity	Cost per unit	Total	Quantity	Cost per unit	Total

ISBN: 9780170229845

b Prepare journal entries (using *general* journal format without narrations).

Albany Electrical
General Journal

Page 1

Date	Particulars	Ref	Dr $	Cr $

c Calculate the cost of microwave ovens sold during June.

ANSWER: Cost of microwave ovens sold = $ _____

2 The following inventory card has been prepared for *Sloggit* tennis racquets in the inventory subsidiary ledger of *Specialty Sports*:

INVENTORY RECORD CARD

Product:	Sloggit	Code No:	4632
Description:	Tennis racquet	Reorder Point:	150
Supplier:	Spiro sports	Reorder Quantity:	300

DATE	PARTICULARS	IN			OUT			BALANCE		
		Quantity	Cost per unit	Total	Quantity	Cost per unit	Total	Quantity	Cost per unit	Total
Mar 1	Balance							200	110	22,000
2	Issue to store				120	110	13,200	80	110	8,800
3	Purchase	300	120	36,000				80	110	8,800
								300	120	36,000
5	Issue to store				50	110	5,500	30	110	3,300
								300	120	36,000
10	Issue to store				30	110	3,300			
					170	120	20,400	130	120	15,600
15	Purchase	300	125	37,500				130	120	15,600
								300	125	37,500
20	Issue to store				130	120	15,600			
					20	125	2,500	280	125	35,000

Specialty Sports is a retail firm that sells sports equipment at stores operating in shopping malls throughout the country. Inventory records are maintained in a central warehouse. Inventory is purchased in bulk from the manufacturers and distributed to the retail stores as required. A perpetual inventory system is used to record all movements of inventory in and out of the warehouse.

Answer the questions below.

a Explain **two** advantages of using the perpetual system to record inventory.

_____

_____

_____

_____

_____

_____

_____

b Explain the meaning of the following terms:

  i reorder point

_____

_____

_____

  ii reorder quantity.

_____

_____

_____

c Calculate the total cost of *Sloggit* racquets issued to stores during March.

ANSWER: Cost of *Sloggit* racquets issued = $ _____

d At the end of March, management assessed the closing inventory of *Sloggit* racquets at $25,000. Explain why management may have made this decision.

_____

_____

_____

_____

e Explain the effect that the remeasurement of inventory will have on the profit for the year ended 31 March.

_____

_____

Accounting – A Next Step

ISBN: 9780170229845

Weighted Average Cost

The second method used to measure inventory is different from the first in that the cost of inventory on hand is *averaged* after each purchase. The inventory card is for paua pendants prepared using this measurement assumption is shown below.

INVENTORY RECORD CARD

Product:	*Paua Pendant*	Code No:	*0129*	
Description:	*Leather strap*	Reorder Point:	*5*	
Supplier:	*Jill's Jewellery*	Reorder Quantity:	*30*	

DATE	PARTICULARS	IN			OUT			BALANCE		
		Quantity	Cost per unit	Total	Quantity	Cost per unit	Total	Quantity	Cost per unit	Total
Oct 1	Balance							5	25.00	125.00
14	Purchases – Jill's Jewellery	10	30.00	300.00				15	28.33	425.00
19	Sales – Te Anau Travel				12	28.33	339.96	3	28.35	85.04
22	Returns – Te Anau Travel	2	28.35	56.70				5	28.35	141.74
31	Purchases – Jill's Jewellery	4	40.00	160.00				9	33.53	301.74

Important!

- After each purchase, the weighted average cost of each item is calculated by dividing the **total cost** by the **total number of items** on hand. For example, after the purchase on 14 October there were 15 items on hand at a total cost of $425.00, which gives a unit cost of ($425.00/15) = $28.33. This price is used to calculate the cost of the goods sold on 19 October.

- When the goods were sold on 19 October, the cost was calculated as 12*$28.33 = $339.96. However, since rounding errors exist in the calculations, the unit cost must be recalculated after every transaction. When the sale has been completed, the total number of units on hand is (15 − 12) = 3. These have a total cost of ($425.00 − 339.96) = $85.04. The unit cost becomes $85.04/3 = $28.35.

- Sales returns are recorded at the same amount as was used when the sale was first recorded.

- Each time a new purchase is made, a new weighted average cost is calculated for the inventory. After the purchase on 31 October, the new cost is ($301.74/9) = $33.53 per unit.

The inventory cards for the other items of inventory under the weighted average cost assumption are shown below.

INVENTORY RECORD CARD

Product:	Kete	Code No:	0133
Description:	Medium	Reorder Point:	5
Supplier:	Flaxworks	Reorder Quantity:	as available

DATE	PARTICULARS	IN			OUT			BALANCE		
		Quantity	Cost per unit	Total	Quantity	Cost per unit	Total	Quantity	Cost per unit	Total
Oct 1	Balance							8	90.00	720.00
3	Sales – Kerikeri Store				6	90.00	540.00	2	90.00	180.00
4	Purchases – Flaxworks	10	90.00	900.00				12	90.00	1,080.00
19	Sales – Te Anau Travel				4	90.00	360.00	8	90.00	720.00
21	Purchases – Flaxworks	4	100.00	400.00				12	93.33	1,120.00
31	Sales – Kerikeri Store				10	93.33	933.30	2	93.35	186.70

INVENTORY RECORD CARD

Product:	Woolly sheep	Code No:	0142
Description:	10 cm	Reorder Point:	10
Supplier:	Colinette's Crafts	Reorder Quantity:	20

DATE	PARTICULARS	IN			OUT			BALANCE		
		Quantity	Cost per unit	Total	Quantity	Cost per unit	Total	Quantity	Cost per unit	Total
Oct 1	Balance							4	20.00	80.00
2	Purchases – Colinette's Crafts	20	20.00	400.00				24	20.00	480.00
4	Returns – Colinette's Crafts				8	20.00	160.00	16	20.00	320.00
15	Sales – Rotorua Souvenirs				10	20.00	200.00	6	20.00	120.00
20	Purchases – Colinette's Crafts	10	22.00	220.00				16	21.25	340.00
25	Sales – Te Anau Travel				8	21.25	170.00	8	21.25	170.00
31	Write-down				8	6.25	50.00	8	15.00	120.00

Important!

- The woolly sheep on hand at the end of the month are written down to the lower of cost and net realisable value. Their weighted average cost was $21.25 each, but due to the fact that a local competitor was selling them for $15, Kiri had decided to sell them for the same price. This represents a reduction in the carrying amount of $6.25 per unit.

- The total inventory write-down using WAC totals $50.00, whereas using FIFO it was $56.00. This is because the two measurement assumptions record the inventory cost at different amounts.

PHOTOCOPYING PROHIBITED
ISBN: 9780170229845

INVENTORY RECORD CARD

Product:	Felt kiwi	Code No:	0145
Description:	Miniature	Reorder Point:	30
Supplier:	Colinette's Crafts	Reorder Quantity:	20

DATE	PARTICULARS	IN			OUT			BALANCE		
		Quantity	Cost per unit	Total	Quantity	Cost per unit	Total	Quantity	Cost per unit	Total
Oct 1	Balance							30	12.00	360.00
2	Purchases – Colinette's Crafts	40	15.00	600.00				70	13.71	960.00
19	Sales – Te Anau Travel				25	13.71	342.75	45	13.72	617.25
20	Purchases – Colinette's Crafts	20	15.00	300.00				65	14.11	917.25
27	Sales – Rotorua Souvenirs				20	14.11	282.20	45	14.11	635.05
31	Drawings – Kiri				4	14.11	56.44	41	14.11	578.61

INVENTORY RECORD CARD

Product:	Tablemat	Code No:	0152
Description:	45 x 30	Reorder Point:	12
Supplier:	Flaxworks	Reorder Quantity:	as available

DATE	PARTICULARS	IN			OUT			BALANCE		
		Quantity	Cost per unit	Total	Quantity	Cost per unit	Total	Quantity	Cost per unit	Total
Oct 1	Balance							25	18.00	450.00
19	Sales – Te Anau Travel				20	18.00	360.00	5	18.00	90.00
21	Purchases – Flaxworks	32	20.00	640.00				37	19.73	730.00
24	Returns – Flaxworks				12	20.00	240.00	25	19.60	490.00
31	Sales – Kerikeri Store				4	19.60	78.40	21	19.60	411.60
	Inventory shortage				1	19.60	19.60	20	19.60	392.00

INVENTORY RECORD CARD

Product:	Paua earrings	Code No:	0160
Description:	Assorted shapes	Reorder Point:	6
Supplier:	Jill's Jewellery	Reorder Quantity:	as available

DATE	PARTICULARS	IN			OUT			BALANCE		
		Quantity	Cost per unit	Total	Quantity	Cost per unit	Total	Quantity	Cost per unit	Total
Oct 1	Balance							6	35.00	210.00
14	Purchases – Jill's Jewellery	10	40.00	400.00				16	38.13	610.00
16	Returns – Jill's Jewellery				2	40.00	80.00	14	37.86	530.00
19	Sales – Te Anau Travel				5	37.86	189.30	9	37.86	340.70
27	Sales – Rotorua Souvenirs				3	37.86	113.58	6	37.85	227.12
29	Returns – Rotorua Souvenirs	1	37.86	37.86				7	37.85	264.98
30	Purchases – Jill's Jewellery	4	40.00	160.00				11	38.64	424.98
31	Error – Jill's Jewellery				4	40.00	160.00	7	37.85	264.98

ISBN: 9780170229845

PHOTOCOPYING PROHIBITED

Inventory Subsystem

Comparison of Measurement Assumptions

The inventory cards in the previous sections represent the **inventory subsidiary ledger**. The **inventory control** accounts provide a useful means of comparing the effects of the two different measurement assumptions on cost of goods sold, closing inventory and the amounts of other transactions that affect inventory. The general ledger accounts are shown in T form and 3-column formats below.

Kiri's Krafts – General Ledger

Inventory control (FIFO) — 130

Date	Particulars	$	Date	Particulars	$
Oct 1	Balance	1,945	Oct 31	Accounts payable	480
31	Accounts payable	4,320		Cost of goods sold	3,826
	Cost of goods sold	100		Drawings	60
				Inventory write-down	56
				Inventory shortage	18
				Balance	1,925
		$6,365			$6,365
Nov 1	Balance	1,925			

Inventory control (WAC) — 130

Date	Particulars	$	Date	Particulars	$
Oct 1	Balance	1,945.00	Oct 31	Accounts payable	480.00
31	Accounts payable	4,320.00		Cost of goods sold	3,909.49
	Cost of goods sold	94.56		Drawings	56.44
				Inventory write-down	50.00
				Inventory shortage	19.60
				Balance	1,844.03
		$6,359.56			$6,359.56
Nov 1	Balance	1,844.03			

Kiri's Krafts – General Ledger

Inventory control (FIFO) — 130

Date	Particulars	Dr $	Cr $	Balance $
Oct 1	Balance			1,945 Dr
31	Accounts payable	4,320		6,265 Dr
	Cost of goods sold		3,826	2,439 Dr
	Cost of goods sold	100		2,539 Dr
	Accounts payable		480	2,059 Dr
	Drawings		60	1,999 Dr
	Inventory write-down		56	1,943 Dr
	Inventory shortage		18	1,925 Dr

Inventory control (WAC) — 130

Date	Particulars	Dr $	Cr $	Balance $
Oct 1	Balance			1,945.00 Dr
31	Accounts payable	4,320.00		6,265.00 Dr
	Cost of goods sold		3,909.49	2,355.51 Dr
	Cost of goods sold	94.56		2,450.07 Dr
	Accounts payable		480.00	1,970.07 Dr
	Drawings		56.44	1,913.63 Dr
	Inventory write-down		50.00	1,863.63 Dr
	Inventory shortage		19.60	1,844.03 Dr

ISBN: 9780170229845

We can compare the results for the two inventory measurement assumptions:

	FIFO	WAC
	$	$
Sales (net)	5,760	5,760.00
Less: Cost of goods sold	3,726	3,814.93
Gross profit	$2,034	$1,945.07
Closing inventory	1,925	1,844.03
Drawings	60	56.44
Inventory write-down	56	50.00
Inventory shortage	18	19.60

> **Note**
>
> The amount for net sales was calculated from the totals of the sales and sales returns and allowances journals:
>
> $5,920 – 160
> = $5,760

In periods of *increasing* prices, the WAC method will give a higher cost of goods sold (hence lower gross profit and closing inventory) than the FIFO method. This is because the FIFO method assumes that all the oldest (cheapest) inventory has been sold, whereas the WAC method includes a proportion of the older prices in its averaging calculation. In periods of *decreasing* prices, the opposite is true.

Many firms prefer the weighted average cost method, especially when the cost of inventory is constantly changing. The FIFO method gives an up-to-date historical cost for inventory in the statement of financial position, but the cost of goods sold is understated in current terms if prices are rising and overstated if prices are falling.

Using the WAC assumption, if prices change evenly and transactions occur evenly throughout the reporting period, both the cost of goods sold and the closing inventory will represent averages for the period. Another advantage of the WAC method is that it lends itself well to computerised accounting systems.

Comparison of Periodic and Perpetual Recording Systems

	Periodic Recording	Perpetual Recording
Recording goods purchased or returned to suppliers	Use purchases account or purchases returns and allowances account	Use inventory account for both types of transaction
Updating inventory balance	Requires stocktake to ascertain quantities and then assign amount based on FIFO or WAC measurement assumption	Records updated after every sale, purchase or other relevant transaction. Measurement assumption decided beforehand.
Recording sales	No affect on inventory account during the reporting period	Inventory and cost of goods sold accounts updated after every transaction
Preparing financial statements	Stocktake required to establish closing inventory so that cost of goods sold can be calculated	Can be prepared at any time using cost of goods sold balance. Stocktake not required before preparing financial statements.
End-of-period stocktake	Required to determine ending inventory and prepare financial statements	Required to identify any missing inventory through comparison with inventory record cards
Identify missing inventory	Not possible since no theoretical record available	Identify through comparison with inventory record cards
Record-keeping	Minimal required as long as records of purchases are kept	Requires records of every item of inventory sold which can be difficult for large businesses selling high volumes of small items unless system is computerised
Reorder point	Visual inspection required to determine stock levels prior to reordering	Reorder point listed on inventory card and can be monitored as card is updated.

Activities

1 **(You should ignore GST in this task.)**

Panda Parties uses a perpetual inventory system. The following information relates to the sale and purchase of burbles for the month of September:

Sep 1 Balance on hand, 2,000 units @ $1.20 each
3 Sold 1,000 units for $3.00 each on credit
10 Purchased 1,000 units @ $1.30 each on credit
13 Cash sale of 1,500 units at $3.20 each
14 Returned 100 faulty units from the purchase on 10 September to the supplier
Purchased 1,600 units @ $1.40 each on credit
20 Sold 1,200 units for $3.50 each on credit
22 Owner took 50 units home for personal use
26 Purchased 1,400 units @ $1.35 each on credit
30 The end-of-month stocktake showed that there were 2,130 units on hand.

Panda Parties

DO THIS!

a Prepare the inventory record card for burbles using each of the following measurement bases:
  i WAC (weighted average cost)
  ii FIFO (first-in first-out).
b Calculate the total sales of burbles for September.
c Complete the table to show the gross profit for September under each of the measurement bases.

a i WAC (Weighted average cost)

INVENTORY RECORD CARD

Product:	Burble	Code No:	9467
Description:	Pink	Reorder Point:	750
Supplier:	Glassco	Reorder Quantity:	1,000

DATE	PARTICULARS	IN			OUT			BALANCE		
		Quantity	Cost per unit	Total	Quantity	Cost per unit	Total	Quantity	Cost per unit	Total

ISBN: 9780170229845

ii FIFO (First-in first-out)

<table>
<tr><td colspan="11" align="center">INVENTORY RECORD CARD</td></tr>
<tr><td colspan="5">Product: Burble</td><td colspan="3">Code No: 9467</td><td colspan="3"></td></tr>
<tr><td colspan="5">Description: Pink</td><td colspan="3">Reorder Point: 750</td><td colspan="3"></td></tr>
<tr><td colspan="5">Supplier: Glassco</td><td colspan="3">Reorder Quantity: 1,000</td><td colspan="3"></td></tr>
</table>

DATE	PARTICULARS	IN			OUT			BALANCE		
		Quantity	Cost per unit	Total	Quantity	Cost per unit	Total	Quantity	Cost per unit	Total

b Calculate the total sales of burbles for September.

ANSWER: Sales = $ _____

c Complete the table below to show the gross profit under each of the measurement bases.

	i	ii
	WAC	**FIFO**
Sales		
Less: **Cost of sales**		
Cost of goods sold		
Inventory shortage		
Cost of sales		
Gross profit		

The inventory card below has been taken from the records of *Wizzle's Toy Extravaganza*:

INVENTORY RECORD CARD

Product:	*Spangles*	Code No:	*327*
Description:	*Gold*	Reorder Point:	*200*
Supplier:	*Metal Merchants*	Reorder Quantity:	*400*

DATE	PARTICULARS	IN			OUT			BALANCE		
		Quantity	Cost per unit	Total	Quantity	Cost per unit	Total	Quantity	Cost per unit	Total
Oct 1	Balance							200	20.00	4,000
3	Sale				100	20.00	2,000	100	20.00	2,000
4	Purchase	200	17.00	3,400				300	18.00	5,400
10	Sale				150	18.00	2,700	150	18.00	2,700
15	Purchase	450	16.00	7,200				600	16.50	9,900
20	Sale				400	16.50	6,600	200	16.50	3,300
28	Purchase	400	15.00	6,000				600	15.50	9,300

The following events have not yet been recorded on the inventory card:
- On 28 October, 100 spangles from that day's order were returned to the supplier because they were faulty.
- On 29 October, it was found that 100 of the 400 items purchased on 28 October had been incorrectly recorded. These were purchases of sprinkles, not spangles.
- The owner took 20 spangles for personal use on 31 October.
- A physical stocktake on 31 October showed that there were 376 units on hand.

DO THIS!

Examine the inventory card above and answer the questions below.

a **Identify** and **describe** the inventory measurement assumption being used by *Wizzle's Toy Extravaganza*.

_____

_____

_____

_____

_____

b Calculate the cost of spangles sold for the month.

ANSWER: Cost of spangles sold = $ _____

c Complete the inventory card above to show the unrecorded events.

d Complete the inventory card on the next page using an alternative measurement assumption.

INVENTORY RECORD CARD

Product: *Spangles* Code No: *327*

Description: *Gold* Reorder Point: *200*

Supplier: *Metal Merchants* Reorder Quantity: *400*

DATE	PARTICULARS	IN			OUT			BALANCE		
		Quantity	Cost per unit	Total	Quantity	Cost per unit	Total	Quantity	Cost per unit	Total

e **Identify** and **describe** the inventory measurement assumption you have used to prepare the inventory card in part **d** above.

_____

_____

_____

_____

f Explain **fully** why the amounts for closing inventory are different on the two inventory cards.

_____

_____

_____

_____

_____

3 The inventory card below has been taken from the records of *Whatsits and Thingummybobs*:

INVENTORY RECORD CARD

Product:	Gizmo	Code No:	1459
Description:	Silver	Reorder Point:	1,500
Supplier:	Handy Gadgets	Reorder Quantity:	1,500

DATE	PARTICULARS	IN			OUT			BALANCE		
		Quantity	Cost per unit	Total	Quantity	Cost per unit	Total	Quantity	Cost per unit	Total
Aug 1	Balance							2,000	2.00	4,000
5	Sale				500	2.00	1,000	1,500	2.00	3,000
10	Purchase	1,500	2.20	3,300				1,500	2.00	3,000
								1,500	2.20	3,300
11	Purchase return				500	2.20	1,100	1,500	2.00	3,000
								1,000	2.20	2,200
16	Sale				800	2.00	1,600	700	2.00	1,400
								1,000	2.20	2,200
18	Sale				600	2.00	1,200	100	2.00	200
								1,000	2.20	2,200
19	Sales return	100	2.00	200				200	2.00	400
								1,000	2.20	2,200
21	Purchase	1,500	2.26	3,390				200	2.00	400
								1,000	2.20	2,200
								1,500	2.26	3,390
25	Sale				200	2.00	400	200	2.20	440
					800	2.20	1,760	1,500	2.26	3,390
31	Shortage				50	2.20	110	150	2.20	330
								1,500	2.26	3,390

The owner of the business keeps his inventory ledger on spreadsheets. He has heard that the weighted average cost assumption for measuring inventory would be easier to operate than the first-in first-out assumption that he is currently using, but he has no idea how to apply it.

DO THIS!

Examine the inventory card above and answer the questions below.

a Explain why the cost of goods sold on 25 October are shown at two different unit costs.

_____

_____

_____

_____

_____

b Explain how the entry on 31 October has arisen.

_____

_____

_____

_____

Accounting – A Next Step  PHOTOCOPYING PROHIBITED   ISBN: 9780170229845

c Complete the inventory card below using **weighted average cost**.

INVENTORY RECORD CARD

Product:	Gizmo	Code No:	1459
Description:	Silver	Reorder Point:	1,500
Supplier:	Handy Gadgets	Reorder Quantity:	1,500

DATE	PARTICULARS	IN			OUT			BALANCE		
		Quantity	Cost per unit	Total	Quantity	Cost per unit	Total	Quantity	Cost per unit	Total

d The selling price of all units during August was $4.00 each (excluding GST). Complete the table below to show gross profit under the two measurement assumptions.

		FIFO	WAC
Sales			
Less:	**Cost of sales**		
	Cost of goods sold		
	Inventory shortage		
Cost of sales			
Gross profit			

e The owner has told you that he is not keen to change from first-in first-out to weighted average cost because his profits would be lower. Explain why this happens and why he does not need to worry about it.

_____

_____

_____

_____

_____

_____

_____

_____

4 **(You should ignore GST in this task.)**
At the end of the reporting period, 31 March 2019, *Glamorous Garments* had 20 satin nightdresses on hand which had cost $70 each and normally retailed at $169.50. After investigating the firm's inventory records, you have discovered the following:

- The cost of nightdresses was measured using the first-in first-out method.
- All the satin nightdresses had been purchased from the same supplier at the same price throughout the year.
- One nightdress which had been returned by a customer was later discovered to be stained with lipstick and is currently offered for sale at $40. This nightdress has been included in the stocktaking figures given above.
- One customer had paid a deposit of $20 on two nightdresses several months earlier but had not returned to collect them. These nightdresses had not been included in the stocktake, but the layby period has now expired and they can be returned to stock.
- The price of four nightdresses in an unpopular style has been reduced to $99.50.

a Complete the inventory card extract below to record any necessary additional information.
b Calculate the closing balance for inventory as it would be shown in the statement of financial position at the end of the reporting period.

a Complete the inventory card extract below to record any necessary additional information.

DATE	PARTICULARS	IN			OUT			BALANCE		
		Quantity	Cost per unit	Total	Quantity	Cost per unit	Total	Quantity	Cost per unit	Total
Mar 31	Balance							20	70	1,400

b Calculate the closing balance for inventory as it would be shown in the statement of financial position at the end of the reporting period.

ANSWER: Closing inventory = $ _____

5 **(You should ignore GST in this question.)**
Value Visuals is a retail store that sells television sets and other home theatre products. The firm records inventory using the perpetual system on the FIFO basis. Two models of television set are for sale: one portable model and a larger, fixed model.
The following details relate to television sets for the six months ended 30 September 2018:

	Portable	Fixed
Inventory on hand at 1 April 2018	25 units @ $300	5 units @ $1,000
Sales	120 units @ $600	36 units @ $1,600
Purchases	$46,900	$37,900
Purchases returns	$7,000	—
Inventory on hand at 30 September 2018	25 units	8 units

Your investigations reveal the following information:

- Sales of all items occurred evenly throughout the six-month period.
- The portable TV sets were purchased on 10 April and 10 July. Each order consisted of 70 units. In April $320 was paid for each unit but in July the price had increased to $350.
- The purchases returns on portable TV sets relate to 20 of the units purchased in July which were found to be faulty and were returned to the supplier on 20 July.

Accounting – A Next Step   PHOTOCOPYING PROHIBITED   ISBN: 9780170229845

- One customer who purchased a portable TV late in July returned it on 4 August and exchanged it for a fixed model. This information has not been incorporated in the figures given above.
- The supplier of the fixed TV sets makes only one delivery per month. Ten units were purchased in on the 20th of the month in each of April, June, August and September. The prices paid were as follows:

20 April	$980	20 August	$950
20 June	960	20 September	900

- Sales for a particular month are recorded at the end of the month, but exchanges and other transactions are recorded on the date that they occur.
- When the stocktake was carried out on 30 September, it was found that one unit of each product had been damaged in the warehouse and as a result these would have to be sold at reduced prices. The fixed set will be sold for $800 and the portable set will be sold for $450.

DO THIS!

Use the information above to answer the questions below.

a Complete the inventory card below for **fixed** TV sets.

INVENTORY RECORD CARD

Product: *TV* Code No: *210*

Description: *Fixed* Reorder Point: *5*

Supplier: *Visaids* Reorder Quantity:

DATE	PARTICULARS	IN			OUT			BALANCE		
		Quantity	Cost per unit	Total	Quantity	Cost per unit	Total	Quantity	Cost per unit	Total

b Complete the inventory card below for **portable** TV sets.

INVENTORY RECORD CARD

Product:	TV	Code No:	200
Description:	Portable	Reorder Point:	5
Supplier:	Visaids	Reorder Quantity:	

DATE	PARTICULARS	IN			OUT			BALANCE		
		Quantity	Cost per unit	Total	Quantity	Cost per unit	Total	Quantity	Cost per unit	Total

6 The table below shows the inventory purchases and (purchases returns) made by *Boys Toys*, a toy wholesaler, in May. (All amounts exclude GST.)

Date	Supplier	Tool set	Hot rod	Robot
May 3	Electrotoys			200 @ $18
7	Major Models		50 @ $45	
7	Electrotoys			(10 @ $18)
15	Kids Stuff	300 @ $32		
18	Kids Stuff	(5 @ $32)		
22	Electrotoys			200 @ $22
25	Major Models		50 @ $50	
30	Kids Stuff	250 @ $30		

 PHOTOCOPYING PROHIBITED

ISBN: 9780170229845

Sales and (sales returns) in units for the same period were:

Date	Tool set	Hot rod	Robot
May 11	25		
12		30	180
20	120		
22	(5)		
28		22	

Opening inventory at May was:

Tool set	Hot rod	Robot
120 @ $35.00	25 @ $42.00	160 @ $17.50

The following events have not yet been recorded:
- The owner took two hot rods and two robots home for his children on 15 May.
- The five tool sets returned by a customer on 22 May had been damaged in the store and were written off on 30 May.
- On 25 May, it was found that *Boys Toys* had been overcharged $2.00 per unit for the robots purchased on 22 May.
- A physical stocktake on 31 May showed the following numbers of units on hand:

Tool set	Hot rod	Robot
520	70	368

- A large chain store has just started selling robots very similar to the ones supplied by *Boys Toys* for $14.99. Customers of *Boys Toys* have advised that the most they will be prepared to pay for these from now on is $10.50 (excluding GST).

a Complete the inventory cards provided using the weighted average cost measurement assumption.
b Explain the reasoning behind any adjustment you have made to the carrying amount of robot inventory on 31 May.

a Complete the inventory cards provided using the **weighted average cost** measurement assumption.

INVENTORY RECORD CARD

Product:	*Tool set*	Code No:	*6453*
Description:	*Deluxe*	Reorder Point:	*100*
Supplier:	*Kids Stuff*	Reorder Quantity:	*300*

DATE	PARTICULARS	IN			OUT			BALANCE		
		Quantity	Cost per unit	Total	Quantity	Cost per unit	Total	Quantity	Cost per unit	Total

ISBN: 9780170229845

INVENTORY RECORD CARD

Product:	Hot rod			Code No:			6592			
Description:	Red			Reorder Point:			50			
Supplier:	Major Models			Reorder Quantity:			50			

DATE	PARTICULARS	IN			OUT			BALANCE		
		Quantity	Cost per unit	Total	Quantity	Cost per unit	Total	Quantity	Cost per unit	Total

INVENTORY RECORD CARD

Product:	Robot			Code No:			7214			
Description:	Silver			Reorder Point:			180			
Supplier:	Electrotoys			Reorder Quantity:			200			

DATE	PARTICULARS	IN			OUT			BALANCE		
		Quantity	Cost per unit	Total	Quantity	Cost per unit	Total	Quantity	Cost per unit	Total

b Explain the reasoning behind any adjustment you have made to the carrying amount of robot inventory on 31 May.

_____

_____

_____

_____

_____

_____

_____

Accounting – A Next Step

PHOTOCOPYING PROHIBITED

ISBN: 9780170229845

Managing Inventory

Inventory represents a significant investment of working capital. Efficient management of inventory is therefore an essential component of the overall management of the firm's assets. There are two aspects to managing inventory: storage and security; and the management of inventory levels.

Storage and Security

Methods of control over storage and security of inventory depend upon the type of business. A retail store, for example, may employ a variety of methods to ensure that inventory does not leave the premises without a sale being recorded. Controls used to prevent theft include:

- Security devices attached to goods, which are removed at point of sale. These devices activate an alarm if an attempt is made to remove them from the store.
- Store detectives who pose as customers and watch for shoplifting and/or visible security staff at the entrance to the store
- Using store-specific packaging and/or sticking the sales docket on the goods so that it can be seen easily
- Disincentives such as notices warning that shoplifters will be prosecuted
- CCTV.

For wholesale and manufacturing businesses, different methods of control are appropriate since most of their goods are stored in warehouses. Customers do not normally collect goods in person – rather goods are shipped either using the firm's own transport or by courier. In these cases, all goods leaving the warehouse must be supported by adequate documentation. This will normally be a sales order from the customer, followed by the completion of a packing slip and invoice as outlined in the accounts receivable subsystem. When a perpetual inventory system is used, inventory records will be updated each time a purchase or sale is made so that periodic checks of the actual inventory against the warehouse records can take place. Any discrepancies can then be investigated.

Managing Inventory Levels

It is very important that the quantity of inventory on hand is managed efficiently and that stock buying policies are appropriate. This means that the correct quantity of inventory should be held – enough to meet demand and maintain faith with customers but not so much as to tie up working capital needlessly. It is only by following good buying policies that the stock turnover for the business will be at an acceptable level.

Managing inventory levels is a balancing act between competing forces:

Excess inventory	Insufficient inventory
• Working capital tied up needlessly, either increasing finance costs or reducing interest that could otherwise be earned from investing surplus cash	• Unable to meet demand from customers, which can lead to customer frustration and loss of trade to competitors
• Increased costs for warehousing and insurance	• For manufacturers, labour costs are paid regardless of productivity. If raw materials are not available, factory staff cannot produce goods for sale and labour costs are fruitless.
• Risk that inventory will become out-of-date or unusable	
• Risk that inventory will be damaged in overcrowded storage facility	

ISBN: 9780170229845

Inventory should be rotated so that older stock is sold first, especially in the case of perishable inventory. Inventory should always be fully insured.

Inventory Purchasing Models

When purchasing inventory (whether raw materials for a manufacturer or finished goods for a retailer), there are some key questions to be answered:

- Which supplier should I use?
- What quantity should I order?
- When do I need to order it?

The **choice of supplier** does not depend only on price. Other, qualitative, factors need to be taken into account such as the quality of goods, regularity of supply, location, quantities available and any quantity discounts that may apply.

The **reorder quantity** depends on a number of factors such as availability, quantity discounts and projected demand as well as ordering costs and available storage space and storage costs.

The **timing of the order** depends upon the lead time necessary (time between order and delivery).

There are several different models that may be used for the ordering of inventory. The most common are described below.

Continuous ordering

This is the model that has been described in previous parts of this module. A standard reorder quantity is used and the order is triggered when inventory levels fall below a preset reorder point. Ordering costs and storage costs are ignored.

Economic order quantity (EOQ)

This is a mathematical model that takes into account the cost of placing an order and the storage costs of holding inventory, as well as the costs of the goods themselves. The formula produces the order quantity that will minimise the total inventory cost.

Both continuous ordering and EOQ models are described as **push** models, where the manufacturer forecasts demand based on past order patterns, then orders raw materials and manufactures the goods. Push models take the risk that the goods manufactured may not be sold due to obsolescence or change in demand, but reduce the risk of running out of inventory (known as a *stock-out*).

Just in time (JIT) model

This model differs from others in that no orders are placed for raw materials until *after* an order has been received from a customer. It is most usually applied to manufacturing or wholesale businesses. Currently this model is used by internet 'daily deal' type businesses who do not order the goods until the deal has closed and they know exactly how many goods have been ordered. However, it is obviously not suitable for normal retail stores.

A firm operating the JIT system effectively has no inventories on hand. Large businesses may receive several shipments per day to maintain supply to their factories. For many firms, this represents a considerable reduction in storage costs, insurance expenses and finance costs since there is very little cash tied up in inventories. The main risk of using the JIT system is that delivery delays will halt production and the workforce will be idle until the raw materials have been received. Some firms maintain a very small inventory and replace this as it is consumed. This variation is known as the *supermarket* model.

JIT is a **pull** model because inventories are ordered on the basis of actual demand from customers, rather than from the manufacturer's own forecasts.

> ### Important!
> Successful operation of a JIT system requires close co-operative relationships with suppliers to ensure that supplies are delivered on time to meet production schedules.

ISBN: 9780170229845

BARCODING: Managing inventory in today's competitive business environment

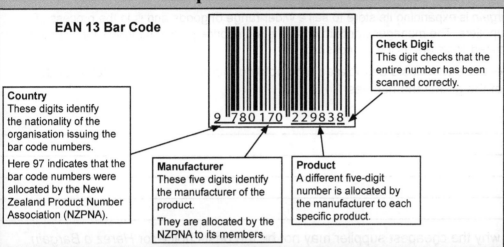

EAN 13 Bar Code

`9 780170 229838`

Country
These digits identify the nationality of the organisation issuing the bar code numbers.

Here 97 indicates that the bar code numbers were allocated by the New Zealand Product Number Association (NZPNA).

Manufacturer
These five digits identify the manufacturer of the product.

They are allocated by the NZPNA to its members.

Product
A different five-digit number is allocated by the manufacturer to each specific product.

Check Digit
This digit checks that the entire number has been scanned correctly.

New Zealand companies are competing in an environment where responsiveness to customers and superior efficiency in relation to competitors can lead to significant competitive advantage. Information is one factor that can be used to improve competitiveness. Information from data that is timely and accurate can assist a business to improve its productivity. Barcode systems can deliver data quickly and accurately and provide cost effective and usable information.

What is a barcode?

A barcode is a visual representation of data that can be read by an optical reader. Traditionally a barcode has been a series of vertical lines and spaces commonly seen on product packaging which are scanned by a barcode reader. The EAN 13 or UPC (Universal Product Code) barcode is attached to, or printed on, consumer products and scanned at the point of sale; for example, in the supermarket each product has a unique UPC which is scanned at the checkout. The price and description is recorded, updating both the store's inventory system and the customer's purchase receipt. These data can be saved and used to build up a database of a customer's purchases and purchasing habits. This infor-

mation can subsequently inform the targeting of promotional programmes.

More recently, 2-D barcodes such as the QR Code (Quick Response Code), comprising black modules within a square, are being used. These are able to contain a large amount of data and, being easily read, are becoming more common. They are often seen in a business's promotional material where they direct a consumer to an internet address. They can be read by a range of devices including smartphones. A QR Code can contain up to 7,089 numeric or 4,296 alphanumeric characters.

The QR Code above will direct you to the NZQA Accounting subject resources web site.

Input

A barcode is not a system in itself but can act as input data for almost any computer system. It enables data to be transferred to a computer to be processed accurately and quickly. In rela-

tion to inventory, the computer can then use this information to update inventory records, track inventory movements through a production system, process a sale and reorder inventory etc.

Efficiency

Barcode data capture eliminates the need for keyboard entry. Barcodes can be easily printed and attached to items of inventory. By attaching a barcode to raw material components, items of work-in-progress or finished goods inventory, the item can be tracked as it moves through a production system from issue ex the raw material store through to customer delivery.

Information input from barcodes has been used to achieve efficiencies such as reducing stocks on hand, increasing labour productivity, improving quality control and speeding up customer delivery times.

Capturing of information through barcode technology is a simple and relatively inexpensive way of monitoring events so that effort may be directed into improving operating efficiencies and customer services.

For interesting information about bar codes and how to calculate the check digit go to: www.makebarcode.com/specs/ean_13.html

---

ISBN: 9780170229845

 PHOTOCOPYING PROHIBITED

Activities

1 *Herez a Bargain* is expanding its store to sell a wider range of goods and is in the process of choosing suppliers. The manager wants to ensure that the price paid to suppliers for inventory and other associated costs are as low as possible.

a Identify and describe **two** costs associated with holding increased inventory levels, other than the cost of the goods themselves.

_____

_____

_____

_____

_____

b Give reasons why the cheapest supplier may not be the best choice for *Herez a Bargain*.

_____

_____

_____

_____

_____

2 *Buy in Bulk* is a food packaging operation that imports large quantities of foodstuffs (such as rice, flour, dried beans and vegetable oils) and repackages them into a range of smaller quantities before reselling them to food manufacturers and fast food franchises. Since the raw materials are imported in extremely large quantities and availability depends upon world-wide growing conditions and shipping schedules, it is not possible to implement a just in time system for the bulk supplies. Packaging materials for each shipment are ordered in advance and held in the factory until the food shipment arrives.

Recently the factory foreman has found that there is always a shortage of some packaging materials, such as large plastic buckets. Investigations have revealed that the only possible explanation is that some staff are pilfering these items from the factory.

a Explain how using a **just in time** system for packaging could help to reduce inventory shortages.

_____

_____

_____

_____

b Explain how using a **just in time** system for packaging could reduce *Buy in Bulk's* annual interest expense.

_____

_____

_____

_____

_____

_____

Accounting – A Next Step

 PHOTOCOPYING PROHIBITED

ISBN: 9780170229845

3 **PART A**

Practical Planters is a small business that manufactures wooden planters of different sizes, suitable for use in home gardens and apartments. Business has been extremely busy in recent months as people have begun to grow more of their own vegetables and fresh herbs for home cooking.

The business is owned by Basil Borage, who works in the factory himself. In the past he has also kept all the accounting records, but demand has increased so much recently that he has had to employ more staff. He has one assistant working full-time in his factory and a yardhand who organises the raw materials both outside in the yard and in a separate small warehouse area. The yardhand takes materials into the workshop area when they are needed. He also helps out in the factory when it is extremely busy.

Basil has also employed a part-time bookkeeper to look after the accounting records, send out invoices to customers and pay all the invoices from suppliers through the firm's internet banking system.

The business handles its raw materials purchases as follows:

- Since the firm uses only a handful of different suppliers, Basil has printed off blank order forms for each supplier. These forms have the suppliers' details on them and these are kept in folders in the factory.
- When raw materials are needed, Basil or his assistant asks the yardhand to bring more into the workshop. If they are running low, whoever has time fills out one of the preprinted order forms, faxes it to the supplier and then throws it away.
- When goods arrive, the yardhand checks them against the packing slip and ticks them off. If the shipment is correct, he puts the packing slip in a file for the bookkeeper. If it is not correct, he gives it to Basil who rings the supplier to sort out the problem. Basil usually puts these packing slips on a spike by his phone until the matter is sorted out and then passes them to the bookkeeper.
- The yardman is responsible for stacking the raw materials, so he puts them in any spare space he can find. Large orders of timber are kept outside in the yard which is secured by a mesh fence. The gate is padlocked each night.
- At the end of each month, the raw materials are counted and Basil works out the cost of them (using the last invoice price) to send to the accountant. *Practical Planters* is having its financial statements prepared monthly at present so that Basil can monitor the effectiveness of his increased staffing levels in relation to the profit generated by expansion of the business.
- All incoming mail is opened by the bookkeeper. When the invoice arrives, she retrieves the packing slip from the file and checks it against the invoice. If everything is in order, she pays the invoice through the internet banking system straight away. She then writes PAID on the invoice and puts it in a file. Each supplier has a separate file. If there is a problem with the invoice, she phones the supplier and puts the invoice aside until the matter is resolved.

Basil has asked for your help because he feels that he is losing control of his business. *Practical Planters* has more than doubled its turnover in the past six months, but the profits and bank balance do not reflect this and Basil wants to know what has gone wrong.

a Basil has complained that the bookkeeper has paid invoices for supplies that the business does not use and has never ordered. Explain how this has happened and what could be done to prevent it.

_____

_____

_____

_____

_____

_____

_____

_____

b When Basil took his records to the accountant, it was found that a number of payments on the bank statement were not supported by any documents.

i Identify **and explain** the internal control weakness that has permitted this situation to arise.

_____

_____

_____

_____

_____

ii Suggest reasons why the payments from the bank have no supporting documentation.

_____

_____

_____

_____

_____

iii Suggest a suitable system that would overcome this situation.

_____

_____

_____

_____

_____

c Basil is finding that, since he has employed staff, the management of raw materials supplies is causing a number of problems. His main concern is that he never knows how much is on hand. Sometimes he receives an urgent order and finds that there are no raw materials to make it, yet he is sure he has ordered them. On the other hand, there are some materials for which there are two or three years' supply in the yard and these are taking up space.

i Suggest possible reasons for the shortage of raw materials Basil is complaining about.

_____

_____

_____

_____

_____

_____

ii Suggest why there are two or three years' supply of some raw materials on hand.

_____

_____

_____

_____

_____

_____

iii Suggest how over-ordering of raw materials could be reduced, using the **current** methods of accounting for inventory.

_____

_____

_____

_____

_____

d Basil has been negotiating a new contract: the supply of planter boxes to a large network of garden centres. However, the buyer for these centres has told him that he must attach bar codes to the planters before any orders will be placed.

Suggest a likely reason that the new customer is insisting on barcode labelling of the planters.

_____

_____

_____

_____

_____

_____

_____

_____

e If Basil is able to negotiate the new contract successfully, _Practical Planters_ will need more staff and a more efficient means of handling supplies of raw materials. Basil is concerned that he may not have sufficient space for an expanded operation. He has considered building an extension to the workshop area but this will reduce the space available in the yard for storage of raw materials. A friend who owns another small manufacturing operation has suggested that Basil adopts a perpetual inventory system and adopts the **just in time** approach to ordering raw materials.

i Explain, _in simple terms that Basil can understand_, what a perpetual inventory system is and how it would operate **for raw materials** at _Practical Planters_.

_____

_____

_____

_____

_____

_____

_____

_____

_____

_____

_____

_____

_____

ISBN: 9780170229845    PHOTOCOPYING PROHIBITED   **Inventory Subsystem**    **69**

ii Explain how a perpetual inventory system would improve the efficiency of raw materials **ordering** at *Practical Planters*.

_____
_____
_____
_____
_____
_____
_____
_____

iii Describe two key features of the **just in time** ordering system.

_____
_____
_____
_____
_____

iv Identify **one** potential **advantage** for *Practical Planters* of using a just in time ordering system for the new contract.

_____
_____
_____
_____
_____

v Identify **one** potential **disadvantage** for *Practical Planters* of using a just in time ordering system for the new contract.

_____
_____
_____
_____
_____

3 **PART B**
(You should ignore GST in this task.)

Basil has asked you to prepare a sample inventory card for one product so that he can understand better how the system might work for *Practical Planters*. He has been through all his source documents and extracted the following information regarding medium-sized metal brackets for July:

Jul 1   Inventory on hand, 2,000 units. Of these, 500 had cost $1.20 and the balance had cost $1.40.
     3   Issued 600 units to the workshop
     7   Purchased 2,000 units @ $1.40 each
     9   Issued 900 units to the workshop
   11   Returned 200 units from the purchase on 7 July to the supplier because they were faulty